CHINA'S ONE-CHILD POLICY: THE GOVERNMENT'S MASSIVE CRIME AGAINST WOMEN AND UNBORN BABIES

HEARING

BEFORE THE

SUBCOMMITTEE ON AFRICA, GLOBAL HEALTH,
AND HUMAN RIGHTS

OF THE

COMMITTEE ON FOREIGN AFFAIRS
HOUSE OF REPRESENTATIVES

ONE HUNDRED TWELFTH CONGRESS

FIRST SESSION

SEPTEMBER 22, 2011

Serial No. 112–105

Printed for the use of the Committee on Foreign Affairs

Available via the World Wide Web: http://www.foreignaffairs.house.gov/

U.S. GOVERNMENT PRINTING OFFICE

68–446PDF   WASHINGTON : 2011

For sale by the Superintendent of Documents, U.S. Government Printing Office
Internet: bookstore.gpo.gov   Phone: toll free (866) 512–1800; DC area (202) 512–1800
Fax: (202) 512–2104   Mail: Stop IDCC, Washington, DC 20402–0001

COMMITTEE ON FOREIGN AFFAIRS

ILEANA ROS-LEHTINEN, Florida, *Chairman*

CHRISTOPHER H. SMITH, New Jersey
DAN BURTON, Indiana
ELTON GALLEGLY, California
DANA ROHRABACHER, California
DONALD A. MANZULLO, Illinois
EDWARD R. ROYCE, California
STEVE CHABOT, Ohio
RON PAUL, Texas
MIKE PENCE, Indiana
JOE WILSON, South Carolina
CONNIE MACK, Florida
JEFF FORTENBERRY, Nebraska
MICHAEL T. McCAUL, Texas
TED POE, Texas
GUS M. BILIRAKIS, Florida
JEAN SCHMIDT, Ohio
BILL JOHNSON, Ohio
DAVID RIVERA, Florida
MIKE KELLY, Pennsylvania
TIM GRIFFIN, Arkansas
TOM MARINO, Pennsylvania
JEFF DUNCAN, South Carolina
ANN MARIE BUERKLE, New York
RENEE ELLMERS, North Carolina
VACANT

HOWARD L. BERMAN, California
GARY L. ACKERMAN, New York
ENI F.H. FALEOMAVAEGA, American Samoa
DONALD M. PAYNE, New Jersey
BRAD SHERMAN, California
ELIOT L. ENGEL, New York
GREGORY W. MEEKS, New York
RUSS CARNAHAN, Missouri
ALBIO SIRES, New Jersey
GERALD E. CONNOLLY, Virginia
THEODORE E. DEUTCH, Florida
DENNIS CARDOZA, California
BEN CHANDLER, Kentucky
BRIAN HIGGINS, New York
ALLYSON SCHWARTZ, Pennsylvania
CHRISTOPHER S. MURPHY, Connecticut
FREDERICA WILSON, Florida
KAREN BASS, California
WILLIAM KEATING, Massachusetts
DAVID CICILLINE, Rhode Island

YLEEM D.S. POBLETE, *Staff Director*
RICHARD J. KESSLER, *Democratic Staff Director*

———

SUBCOMMITTEE ON AFRICA, GLOBAL HEALTH, AND HUMAN RIGHTS

CHRISTOPHER H. SMITH, New Jersey, *Chairman*

JEFF FORTENBERRY, Nebraska
TIM GRIFFIN, Arkansas
TOM MARINO, Pennsylvania
ANN MARIE BUERKLE, New York

DONALD M. PAYNE, New Jersey
KAREN BASS, California
RUSS CARNAHAN, Missouri

CONTENTS

CHINA'S ONE–CHILD POLICY: THE GOVERNMENT'S MASSIVE CRIME AGAINST WOMEN AND UNBORN BABIES

THURSDAY, SEPTEMBER 22, 2011

House of Representatives,
Subcommittee on Africa, Global Health,
and Human Rights
Committee on Foreign Affairs,
Washington, DC.

The subcommittee met, pursuant to notice, at 2 p.m., in room 2200, Rayburn House Office Building, Hon. Christopher H. Smith (chairman of the subcommittee) presiding.

Mr. SMITH. The subcommittee will come to order. And we are awaiting the arrival of my distinguished colleague Don Payne, who will be here shortly, as well as our other members, who will be here shortly as well.

I want to thank you for coming to this extremely important hearing as we examine the consequences of some 33 years of China's implementation of this one-child-per-couple policy. China's one-child policy is state-sponsored cruelty and constitutes massive crimes against humanity. Indeed, the Nuremberg Nazi war crimes tribunal properly construed forced abortion as a crime against humanity.

Nothing in human history compares to the magnitude of China's 33-year assault on women and children. Today in China, rather than being given maternal care, pregnant women, without birth-allowed permits, are hunted down and forcibly aborted. They are mocked, belittled, and humiliated. There are no single moms in China, except those who somehow evade the family planning cadres and conceal their pregnancy. For over three decades, brothers and sisters have been illegal; a mother has absolutely no right to protect her unborn baby from state-sponsored violence.

Over the years, I have chaired 29 congressional human rights hearings focused in whole or in part on China's one-child-per-couple policy. At one, the principal witness, Wuijan, a Chinese student attending a U.S. university, testified how her child was forcibly murdered by the government. She said, and I quote, in part, "The room was full of moms who had just gone through a forced abortion. Some moms were crying. Some moms were mourning. Some moms were screaming. And one mom was rolling on the floor with unbearable pain." Then Wuijan said it was her turn, and through her tears she described what she called her "journey in hell."

(1)

We will be hearing the testimony of other victims of forced abortion today, and we are extremely grateful to them for joining us. Not only does it take a great deal of courage to share what must be one of the most painful experiences of their lives, but they are also speaking truth to power, a Chinese Government that may well retaliate not only against them, if given the opportunity, but also against family members who may still be in China. Again, we thank them for sharing their very, very sad and tragic stories.

Women bear the major brunt of the one-child policy not only as mothers. Due to male preference in China's society and the limitation on the family size to one child, the policy has directly contributed to what is accurately described as gendercide, the deliberate extermination of a girl, born or unborn, simply because she happens to be female.

As a result of the Chinese Government's barbaric attack on mothers and their children, the U.S. State Department estimated a full 10 years ago that there may be 100 million more males than females in China today. It has been noted that the three most dangerous words in China are "It's a girl."

In July, I offered an amendment demanding the release and an end to the torture of the Chinese defense attorney Chen Guangcheng, who bravely defended forced abortion victims in China. Both Chen and his wife Yuan Weijing are at risk of dying from repeated beatings by the Chinese secret police and refused access to critically needed medical care.

In the latter part of August when Vice President Joe Biden visited China, he stated that he "fully understood" the one-child policy, and that he is not "second-guessing" it. His words. Can you imagine what the public reaction would be if the Vice President of the United States said that he fully understands and is not second-guessing copyright infringement or gross violations of intellectual property rights? When it comes to things, when it comes to products, there would be a huge cry from the United States if the Vice President were to say that he fully understands that kind of violation of rights. Not so when it comes to women who are being degraded and humiliated, and their children destroyed, and their lives destroyed.

It is worth noting that the World Health Organization suggested there are some 500 women per day—not per week, per month, but per day—who commit suicide. Attributable—we don't know what to extent—but clearly by the anecdotal information—in large part to the terrible deprivations that are imposed on them through forced abortion, of having their children literally stolen from them and then killed by the state.

The one-child-per-couple policy is the most egregious systematic attack on mothers ever. For my Vice President to publicly state that he fully understands the one-child policy and then say he won't second-guess it is unconscionable and sells out every mom in the PRC who has suffered from this abuse. Instead of defending the one-child policy, Vice President Biden should have asked for the release of Chen and his wife Yuan, or at least made a formal request to see them.

Although Vice President Biden attempted to backtrack on his extraordinarily callous comment about the policy, his record in the

U.S. Senate shines a spotlight on his long-held disregard for the severity of this human rights violation. On September 13, 2000, he joined 52 other Senators in defeating an amendment by then-Senator Jesse Helms condemning the one-child policy. I would note parenthetically that 15 years before, I offered a very similar amendment. It passed unanimously in the House. It didn't pass in the Senate. And then-Senator Biden reportedly blocked it because he was concerned that condemning China on fundamental human rights would interfere with the normalization of trade relations.

I would note parenthetically that when President Clinton linked human rights, including the issue of forced abortion, in 1993 as a condition of Most Favored Nation status. I was at the lead of the pack defending the President, a Democrat President, for listing human rights and linking it to our trading policy with the PRC. Sadly, on May 26, 1994, he delinked those human rights on a Friday afternoon, and only David Bonior, Nancy Pelosi—not yet Speaker—and I held press conferences saying, how could you delink human rights and throw the people of China, who aspire to freedom and democracy and human rights, under the bus?

I invited the Vice President to join us at this hearing to explain his full understanding of the one-child policy. I have been informed that he is not in DC today and could not attend. Given the grave importance of this issue and literally millions of lives at stake, I extend to the Vice President an open invitation to testify at a hearing at his convenience to share his "understanding" with the subcommittee and what actions, if any, the Obama administration will take in ending this barbaric policy.

I would note that he was the chairman of the Foreign Relations Committee—and I have served with him for years. Our careers have coincided. I offered the first amendment ever on the forced abortion policy back on May 9, 1984, and filled the record with documentation, much of it Chinese documentation, some of it from the Frontline and 60 Minutes pieces that were done, some that were in the Washington Post. There is no doubt that we knew even then how horrific this policy was. Unfortunately, he says that he fully understands this and is not going to second-guess it.

I also asked Secretary of State Hillary Clinton at a hearing on March 1 of this year whether or not she or President Obama raised the issue of coerced abortion and gendercide in China directly in the face-to-face meeting with Hu Jintao when he was here in Washington. Chai Ling and Reggie Littlejohn will remember because we held a press conference imploring, pleading with the President to raise this issue in his face-to-face meetings and in any press conference which he had later on that week with Hu Jintao. Not a word, not a word was uttered in a state dinner; instead lavishing praise was heaped upon Hu Jintao, who oversees a gulag state. Not a word about any of this. Secretary Clinton said she didn't know; she refused to answer the question, but would get back to us. We are still waiting. That was March 1. We still have not heard a word about whether or not the President raised this.

Democrat or Republican, I don't care who is in the White House, we have a duty, I believe, to raise human rights with dictatorship and not lose that opportunity.

I read the People's Daily the day after Hu Jintao was at the White House. It was filled with praise from the U.S. President, filled with praise from the U.S. Government about Hu Jintao's dictatorship. So they certainly were not held to account in any way, shape, or form.

Not only is the current administration turning a blind eye to the atrocities being committed under the one-child-per-couple policy, but it has even contributed financial support, contrary to U.S. law, through the UNFPA. As I said 27 years ago, on May 9, 1984, I offered the first foreign aid amendment to deny funding to any organization—I don't care who it is—that in any way supports or co-manages a coercive population-control program. Voluntary, yes, but not involuntary, not coercive. And unfortunately we have not seen this administration step up to the plate. As a matter of fact, we have provided over $50 million per year to the UNFPA and nary a concern expressed about the women who are suffering.

I asked Wei Jingsheng, the father of the democracy movement, at a hearing like this, after he got out of prison, what he thought about the UNFPA's complicity in forced abortion in China, and he said it was an abomination and went on and on to say that to have the U.N. working hand in glove with the state family planning cadres in oppressing women is unthinkable, and yet it is the reality.

I would point out that in June 2008, Deputy Secretary of State John Negroponte notified Congress under the previous administration, that the UNFPA was denied funding because—and he said this—because it provided financial and technical resources through its sixth cycle China Country Program to the National Population and Family Planning Commission and related agencies. He also pointed out that the UNFPA and all foreign organizations operating there fully comply, adhere to Chinese law. So they follow what is prescribed by the State Family Planning Council and then adhere to it and implement that very policy that so injures and hurts women.

On one of my several trips to Beijing, I challenged Peng Peiyun, then China's director of the nation's population control program, to end the coercion, and we had a very robust debate. Madam Peng told me that the UNFPA was very supportive of the one-child-per-couple policy and repeatedly said that they say there is no coercion. So how could I be raising the issue when this organization had so whitewashed and presented for all comers and all critics that it is a totally voluntary program? As a matter of fact, for 30 years, UNFPA has heaped praise on China's program, again, to the detriment of the women who have suffered so egregiously.

I also am concerned—and I will conclude with this and then go to our very distinguished witnesses who are here today—that the program of China is also being exported. There was a group of sub-Saharan African health ministers invited a couple years ago to learn the blessings of child limitation, China style. And even Paul Kagame of Rwanda has said he wants a three-child-per-couple policy so that they can reap the economic benefits that China has reaped. And unfortunately, you only get there through coercion.

And I will say to our witnesses—and I am so grateful for them all being here—that your witness today—you know, I have read Bare Branches. I read it soon after it came out, Dr. Hudson, and it raised a whole new area that Congress needs and anyone of concern needs to take seriously about the consequences to the fabric of society in China, the gangs that are already forming but will only get worse as time goes on. Men will not be able to find wives. I know we have different estimates, no one knows for sure, but Chinese demographers suggests that by 2020, 40 million men will not be able to find wives. They have been exterminated through this anti-girl policy and anti-woman policy. And the impacts, even in a larger context, to nearby countries and really the world, is very, very significant in terms of potential war. And I know you make that point so clearly in the book.

I would now turn to our witnesses, beginning first with Ms. Ji Yeqing, who was born in 1975, grew up in a small town outside of Shanghai. After completing high school, she worked in an automobile assembly plant. She married her husband in 1996 and had a daughter the following year. Her peaceful life, however, was shattered after two forced abortions in 2003 and 2006. Along with the implementation, involuntarily, of an IUD, these violations took a grave toll on her body and on her marriage, which ended in 2008. Ms. Ji escaped to the United States in October of last year and has since remarried and will tell her story in a moment.

And then we will be hearing secondly, testifying under a pseudonym behind a closed area, and that will be Ms. Liu Ping, who was born in Tianjin, China, in 1958. Because of the Cultural Revolution, she was unable to finish school. She and her husband married in 1981, just after the one-child-per-couple policy began. As a worker in a textile factory, she was forced by the Family Planning Commission to undergo five abortions. She came to the U.S. in 1999 and lives with her husband in New England. Ms. Liu has one son and also lives in the United States. Her dream is to finish her education and return to school. She is behind that barrier to prevent retaliation against her family in China.

Ms. Ji, and then I will go to our other witnesses momentarily.

STATEMENT OF MS. JI YEQUIG, VICTIM OF FORCED ABORTION

[The statement and answers of Ms. Ji were delivered through an interpreter.]

Ms. JI. Mr. Chairman Smith and honorable Members of Congress, my name is Ji Yeqing. I was born December 2, 1975, in Jiading, Shanghai. I married Liu Bin in Shanghai in October 1996. My daughter Liu Yiyang was born on September 7, 1997. After she was born, the family planning agencies ordered me to go to the hospital and have an IUD inserted into my uterus after I was done nursing my child. At that time, my husband and I both wanted another child. My in-laws also had a very strong bias against girls and urged us to have a son. As a result, I did not go to the hospital for the IUD.

My husband and I decided then we would wait to have a second child until our daughter was old enough to attend kindergarten. I would then have time and energy to take care of the children. So I bought pills every month from the pharmacy for contraception. When the child was 4 and in kindergarten, we stopped the contraception.

In June 2003, I discovered that I was pregnant again after a checkup at the only gynecologist clinic nearby, the Jiading District Women and Children's Clinic. Both my husband and I were very happy. However, the clinic was in close cooperation with the Family Planning Commission of Xiaomiao Village, Jiading District of Shanghai, and reported my pregnancy. The day after my checkup at the clinic, Li Chunping of the Family Planning Commission and three other agents came to our home and told me that, according to China's one-child policy, we could not have a second child. I was pregnant again. I had no choice but to undergo an abortion; otherwise, we would be sabotaging the family planning policy and breaking the law. Not only would we be fined 200,000 yuan, equivalent to $31,300, which was more than three times our combined annual income, but also, we would be fired from our jobs. We were very afraid at the time of losing our jobs. We could never acquire enough money to pay the exorbitant fines.

Li then brought me to the same clinic to force an abortion. After that operation, they made me promise that I would have the IUD put in. I told them I would do it after my body recovered. Only then did they release me.

But I never did get the IUD implemented because I was still very hesitant about the IUD procedure. I had heard it was very painful, and it could produce serious physical complications. So I continued taking contraceptive pills. My in-laws insisted that we try for another pregnancy. They also promised to give us money to pay for the fines. They wanted a grandson, even if it would cost 200,000 yuan.

My husband persuaded me to stop taking the pills in February 2006. I was pregnant again in September of the same year. We were determined to have another child and prepared for the fines. After my checkup at the hospital, like the previous time, the Family Planning Commission learned of it the very next day. We had known of the close cooperation between the clinic and the local birth-planning agencies, so we expected this. But there was only one licensed hospital in that area, so we had no choice but to go there for checkups.

Two days after my visit to the hospital, Li Chunping and five other agents came to our home to ask why I had not had the IUD inserted and why I had decided to get pregnant again. I told them that I wanted another child, and we were prepared to pay for the fine. Li stated that Chinese law decreed that the second child was forbidden. Even after it was born, the child could not be registered and would not be able to attend school. More than the fines, we would be fired from our jobs with a child that would never be registered by the census. But by this time, we were not afraid. We were willing to take the punishment of fines and losing our jobs. It wasn't as important as for us to have our child again.

Li then ordered the other agents to bring me to the hospital for a forced abortion. They surrounded us. Li and two others grabbed me by the arm and dragged me outside. Two others stopped my husband Liu Bin from rescuing me and started beating him. I begged them to spare us. We only wanted another baby. I never wanted to do anything evil. Why did they keep such a close watch over us? I also said we were willing and prepared to pay the fine.

I kept begging them in tears, but it was no use. Then I threatened to take legal action, but Li replied that my pregnancy with the second child was illegal already, so reporting the case to the court would be useless.

I could not free myself, although I struggled all the way. They dragged me down from the fourth floor into a waiting car and then drove me into Jiading Women and Children's Clinic and pulled me directly into the operating room. Li held me down in the bed and sedated me. The abortion was performed while I was unconscious. When I came to, I was already in the recovery room outside the operating room. Doctors told me that they had inserted the IUD immediately after the abortion, and that I was responsible for the cost of the IUD procedure. So the IUD was installed inside me against my will while I was laying unconscious, completely unaware and unable to defend myself.

After the abortion I felt empty, as if something was scooped out of me. My husband and I had been so excited for our new baby. Now suddenly all that hope and joy and excitement disappeared, all disappeared in one instant. I was very depressed and despondent. For a long time, whenever I thought about my lost child, I would cry.

After the IUD insertion, my body continued to feel discomfort, frequently with back pain. I wanted the IUD taken out, but the hospital never allowed it. Removal of the IUD required a stamped permission from the Family Planning Commission. When I went to the Family Planning Commission, Li Chunping was very determined in her refusal. She said that physical reactions to the IUD were normal, and there was no need to panic. Removal of the IUD was impossible for me.

After 2 years of living with that pain, my in-laws gave up hopes that they would have a grandson through me. They began pressuring my husband to divorce me. At that time my husband had also started to change. He frequently stayed away from home for several nights. When I tried to reason with him, he said that since I had not given him a son, he would find someone else who would. I felt desperate. I lost all hope and confidence in my marriage. At the end of 2008, in tears, I signed the divorce agreement Liu Bin handed to me. And so my first marriage ended after a great deal of suffering.

I met my current husband Gong Xiaolin in 2009, married him in October 2010, and then came with him to the United States. We would love to have another child together. Upon arrival in the U.S., I went to a clinic to remove my IUD and to receive a gynecological exam. The doctor told me that I had cervical erosion, likely due to the poor medical conditions of my forced abortions.

We realize how lucky we are to be in America where there is no fear of the Family Planning Commission, and women have the choice to keep their babies. Today I am able to tell my story for the first time. It is my prayer that the one-child policy will come to an end soon and set the Chinese people free from this awful oppression. Thank you very much for your time and attention.

[The prepared statement of Ms. Ji follows:]

Yeqing Ji's Testimony Before Congress
September 22, 2011

Mr. Chairman and honorable Members of Congress,

My name is Ji Yeqing. I was born on December 2, 1975, in Jiading, Shanghai. I married Liu Bin in Shanghai in October 1996. My daughter, Liu Yiyang, was born on September 7, 1997. After she was born, the Family Planning agencies ordered me to go to the hospital and have an intrauterine device (IUD) inserted into my uterus after I was done nursing my child. At the time, my husband and I both wanted another child. My in-laws also had very strong biases against girls and urged us to have a boy. As a result, I did not go to the hospital for the IUD.

My husband and I decided then that we would wait to have a second child until after our daughter was old enough to attend kindergarten. I would then have time and energy to take care of the children. So I bought pills every month from the pharmacy for contraception. When the child was four and in kindergarten, we stopped the contraception. In June 2003, I discovered that I was pregnant again after a checkup at the only gynecological clinic nearby, the Jiading District Women and Children's Clinic. Both my husband and I were very happy. However, the clinic was in close cooperation with the Family Planning Commission of Xiaomiao Village, Jiading District of Shanghai and reported my pregnancy. The day after my checkup at the clinic, Li Chunping of the Family Planning Commission and three other agents came to our home and told me that according to the One-Child Policy, we could not have a second child. I was pregnant again and had no choice but to undergo an abortion. Otherwise, we would be sabotaging the Family Planning Policy and breaking the law. Not only would we be fined 200,000 yuan ($31,300), which was more than three times our combined annual income, but also we would be fired from our jobs. We were very afraid at the time about losing our jobs. We could never acquire enough money to pay the exorbitant fines. Li then brought me to the same clinic to force an abortion. After the operation, they made me promise that I would have the IUD put in. Only then did they release me.

But I never did get the IUD implanted because I was still very hesitant about the IUD procedure. I had heard it was very painful and could produce serious physical complications. So I continued taking contraceptive pills. My in-laws insisted that we try for another pregnancy. They also promised to give us money to pay for the fines. They wanted a grandson even if it cost 200,000 yuan. My husband persuaded me to stop taking the pills in February 2006. I was pregnant again in September of the same year. We were determined to have another child and prepared for the fines. After my checkup at the hospital, like the previous time, the Family Planning Commission learned of it the very next day. We had known of the close cooperation between the clinic and the local birth planning agencies, so we expected this. But there was only one licensed hospital in the area, so I had no choice but to go there for checkups. Two days after my visit to the hospital, Li Chunping and five other agents came to our home to ask why I had not had the IUD inserted and why I had decided to get pregnant again. I told them that I wanted another child and we were prepared to pay the fines. Li stated that Chinese law decreed that the second child was forbidden. Even if it was born, the child could not be registered and would not be able to attend school. More than the fines, we would be fired from our jobs with a child that would never be registered by the census. But this time we were not afraid. We were willing to take the punishment of fines and losing our jobs. It wasn't as important to us as our child.

Li then ordered the other agents to bring me to the hospital for an abortion. They surrounded us. Li and two others grabbed me by the arm and dragged me outside. Two others stopped my husband Liu Bin from rescuing me and beat him. I begged them to spare us. We only wanted another baby and never wanted to do anything evil. Why did they keep such close watch over us? I also said we were willing and prepared to pay the fines. I kept begging them in tears, but it was no use. Then I threatened to take legal action, but Li replied that my pregnancy with a second child was illegal, so reporting the case to court would be useless. I couldn't free myself although I struggled all the way. They dragged me down from the fourth floor into a waiting car, drove into the Jiading Women and Children's Clinic, and pulled me directly into the operating room. They held me down in a bed and sedated me. The abortion was performed while I was unconscious. When I came to, I was already in the recovery room outside the operating room. Doctors told me that they had installed the IUD immediately after the abortion, and that I was responsible for the cost of the IUD procedure. So, the intrauterine device was installed in me against my will while I was lying unconscious, completely unaware. After the abortion, I felt empty, as if something was scooped out of me. My husband and I had been so excited for our new baby. Now, suddenly, all that hope and joy and excitement had disappeared, all in an instant. I was very depressed and despondent. For a long time, whenever I thought about my lost child, I would cry.

After the IUD insertion, my body continued to feel discomfort, with frequent back pains. I wanted the IUD taken out, but the hospital never allowed it. Removal of the IUD required a stamped permission from the Family Planning Commission. When I went to the Family Planning Commission, Li Chunping was very determined in her refusal. She said that physical "reactions" to the IUD was normal and there was no need to panic. Removal of the IUD was impossible for me. After two years of living with this pain, my in-laws gave up hope that they would have a grandson through me. They began pressuring my husband to divorce me. At that time, my husband also started to change. He frequently stayed away from home for several nights. When I tried to reason with him, he said that since I had not given him a son, he would find someone else who could. I felt desperate and lost all hope or confidence in my marriage. At the end of 2008, in tears, I signed the divorce agreement Liu Bing handed to me. And so my first marriage ended after a great deal of suffering.

I met my current husband, Gong Xiaolin, in 2009, married him in October 2010, and then came with him to the United States. We would love to have a child together. Upon arrival in the U.S., I went to a clinic to remove my IUD and to receive a gynecological exam. The doctor told me that I had cervical erosion, likely due to the poor medical conditions of my forced abortions.

We realize just how lucky we are to be in the U.S., where there is no fear of a Family

Planning Commission and women have the choice to keep their babies. Today I am able to tell my story for the first time. It is my prayer that the One-Child Policy will come to an end soon and set the Chinese people free from this awful oppression. Thank you very much for your time and attention.

Mr. SMITH. Ms. Ji, thank you very much for your very brave testimony to the subcommittee today. I wish everyone in America could hear what you just said. So thank you so very, very much.

Mr. Fortenberry. Our vice chairman, Jeff Fortenberry, is here. Thank you.

Mr. FORTENBERRY. Thank you, Mr. Chairman.

Ms. Ji, let me echo the sentiments of our chairman in expressing our heartfelt horror as to what has happened to you, but also a heartfelt embrace that you are now welcome in a country that is trying to struggle with this issue of respecting unborn human life. But at least we haven't slipped into this barbaric practice of having families subjected to the strong arm of the government coming in and asking them how many children that they have; if they have more than one, saying that is more than one too many.

I am deeply grieved by your story, and yet at the same time touched by your willingness to come here and share this with us. And I agree with the chairman. If you would indulge us further with your courage and continue to speak out boldly, you will greatly assist those of us who are trying to join in solidarity as a human family and say this type of barbaric practice must be stopped, it cannot exist in a world that is going to call itself civilized, and recognize the reality of the pain and difficulty it has caused on people like you.

So I want to personally thank you for coming and saying this in a most courageous way, for your forthrightness, but also to give you a warm embrace as a new American in a country where we have the chance to stop this type of pernicious activity because of our beliefs in the rights and dignity of all. We are still living that out imperfectly in our own laws, yet at the same time we haven't slipped this far.

As I was listening to you, I turned my tie over just to see if it was made in China or not. And fortunately, it wasn't. But I would recommend to all of you, the next time you pick something up to buy, look at where it is made. How are we indirectly perhaps cooperating in propping up a system that does this to its own people in the name of economic progress? Economic progress is about persons, not about regimes who are going to do this to the citizens of their own country.

So, Mr. Chairman, I am sorry to interject what is more like an opening statement. And I am sorry to take away your time, the rest of the witnesses. But I was just simply compelled by Ms. Ji's story and wanted to publicly thank you.

Mr. SMITH. Thank you very much, Mr. Vice Chairman.

We will now recognize Ms. Liu, who I said at the outset was compelled, was forced, was coerced into having five abortions. And for reasons of protecting her extended family in China, she is behind that barrier.

Ms. Liu.

STATEMENT OF MS. LIU PING, VICTIM OF FORCED ABORTION

Ms. LIU. Thank you, Mr. Chairman. And thank you, Congressman Fortenberry. I am really honored to be here to have the opportunity to testify today before Congress to expose to America and the world how the one-child policy in China destroys lives and the rights of women.

My name is Liu Ping. I was born in 1958 in Tianjin, China, and arrived in the United States in 1999. Before coming to America, I worked in a state-owned textile factory in Tianjin. The majority of the workers in the factory were women, many of whom were also of reproductive age, so the family planning policy was implemented especially strictly. I am just one of those many, many women whose lives were destroyed by this policy.

I married my husband in 1981. In September 1983, we gave birth to a boy. According to the policy at that time, a woman who gave birth was required to implement an IUD, or one of the spouses was required to undergo a sterilization operation. At that time I had swelling in my right kidney for undiagnosed reasons, so doctors refused to implement the IUD in me and recommended instead I use other methods for contraception. Without the IUD, I became a prime target for surveillance by the factory's Family Planning Commission.

From 1983 to 1990, because of the one-child policy, I had to undergo five forced abortions on the following dates: September 28, 1984; December 17, 1985; March 20, 1986; May 5, 1989; and December 14, 1990. All the operations were recorded in my medical history. I suffered greatly at the hands of the inhumane one-child policy.

In the 1980s, shortly after implementation of the one-child policy in China, there were many severe methods of surveillance and punishment to prevent unplanned pregnancies and above-quota births. My factory's Family Planning Commission used three levels of control: At the factory level, in the factory clinic, and on the factory floor. There was a system of collective punishment. If one worker violated the rules, all workers would be punished. Workers monitored each other. Women of reproductive age can account for 60 percent of my factory floor. Colleagues were suspicious and hostile to each other because of the one-child policy. Two of my pregnancies were reported by my colleagues to the Family Planning Commission.

When discovered, pregnant women would be dragged to undergo forced abortions. There was simply no other choice. We had no dignity as potential child-bearers. By order of the factory's Family Planning Commission, every month during our menstrual period, women had to undress in front of the birth-planning doctor for examination. If anyone escaped the examination, she would be forced to take a pregnancy test at the hospital. We were only allowed to collect a salary after it was confirmed that we were not pregnant.

The day of my fifth and last abortion, December 14, 1990, was the saddest day of my life. Because I was not able to prove that I wasn't pregnant within the 10- to 15-day period, the birth-planning doctor in the factory clinic found out about my pregnancy. That day officials from the factory's Family Planning Commission forced me to be driven to the City Police Hospital and forced me to have an abortion in the birth-planning department. It was my first operation in that hospital. All my previous abortions took place in the Central City Hospital.

I did not know what officials in my factory told the doctors. After the abortion, the doctors, without my knowledge, implanted a metal IUD in my body. When I learned of the procedure, I protested that I had a kidney disease and could not keep the IUD, but they completely ignored me. The doctor just gave the bill to my husband and told him to pay. While my husband argued with the doctors, I was recovering in the hospital bed. When I left the operating room, still weak, I could not find my husband. I was told that he was arrested. I collapsed crying from the physical toll of the two operations and the emotional shock. A kind nurse tried to comfort me somewhat, but she was shooed away by a man who also threatened to have me arrested by the police.

By this time, the family planning officials who dragged me to the hospital were nowhere to be found. I felt alone, sick, and weak. Afterwards, I learned that my husband had been sentenced to criminal detention without a trial for violating and obstructing the one-child policy, disturbing the normal operations of the hospital, and disturbing social peace. Fifteen days later, my husband was finally released and returned home.

I was in great pain from the medical IUD and the weakness of the abortion and almost did not want to live. The arrest of my husband deprived me of the care of my family. My young child did not know what was happening and kept crying for his father. I did not know what to do and could only hold my son and cry with him.

Even now, when I think of all this, my heart still breaks, and I feel the pain all over again. Those painful 15 days of separation became the catalyst of my eventual failed marriage. My body suffered great damage from all those five forced abortions. I gradually grew afraid of family life with my husband. I tried to find excuses to refuse any intimacy demands from my husband. I grew to hate him after the IUD was inserted because I blamed my sufferings on him, on his unwillingness to be surgically sterilized. He had known of my kidney disease, but would not make any sacrifice for me, and, therefore, he didn't love me.

After the fifth abortion and the IUD insertion, my factory also gave me a serious administrative warning and fined me 6 months wages. Afterwards I had to go to the factory clinic every month for exams to make certain that I had not privately taken out the IUD nor became pregnant again. I carried this IUD in my body for over a decade before I finally came to America.

My husband's detention accelerated the demise of our marriage. He was suspended from his job and forced to write letters of regret, and then eventually fired from his job in 1991. Our family immediately sunk into financial difficulties. Arguments and fights became a common thing every day. I was laid off at the end of 1995.

As I was still considered of reproductive age, the Family Planning Commission of my neighborhood committee took up the job of monitoring me. In early 1997, I spent 40 days taking care of my terminally ill and dying mother and missed the monthly pregnancy check. Agents from the Family Planning Commission waited at my home to drag me to the exam. When they pushed me to the ground, I fell and hurt my neck vertebrae. My spirit completely collapsed after this one. I attempted suicide, but was stopped by my family from jumping.

With the help of old friends, in 1999, I escaped the country that humiliated me and tormented me and came to the free soil of America. My husband came to the U.S. a year later. We were unable to mend our past grievances and divorced in 2001. I became extremely depressed and suffered severe depression after the divorce, but at the suggestion of my friends, I started attending church, where I felt the warmth of Christ's body. The Lord Jesus led me to give up the bitterness in my heart piece by piece.

In 2009, my neck injury flared up again. My ex-husband came to take care of me and eventually joined with me. After I was baptized last year, our marriage was able to be reconciled again. Now I live in the great family of Christ in the free land of America. I feel happiness and joyful. But I know in my homeland, China, there are millions of women who are suffering, as I did. Each day thousands of young lives are being destroyed. I beg everyone to save them. I invite all to join with me in prayers for them.

Let the love of our Heavenly Father, the grace of our Lord Jesus and the Holy Spirit fill their hearts and free them from the hell they are living on earth. In the name of our Lord Jesus, we pray. Amen. Thank you.

[The prepared statement of Ms. Liu follows:]

Ping Liu's Testimony Before Congress
September 22, 2011

Mr. Chairman and honorable Members of Congress,

I am very grateful for the opportunity to testify today before Congress to expose to America and the world how the One-Child Policy in China destroys lives and the rights of women.

My name is Liu Ping. I was born in 1958 in Tianjin, China, and arrived in the United States in 1999. Before coming to America, I worked in a state-owned textile factory in Tianjin. The majority of the workers in the factory were women, many of whom were also of reproductive age, so the Family Planning Policy was implemented especially strictly. I am simply one of these many women whose lives were destroyed by the policy.

I married my husband in 1981. In September 1983, I gave birth to a boy. According to the policy at that time, women who gave birth were required to have intrauterine devices (IUD's) implanted, or one of the spouses was required to undergo a sterilization operation. At that time I had swelling in my right kidney for undiagnosed reasons, so doctors refused to implant the IUD in me and recommended instead that I use other contraceptive methods. Without the IUD, I became the prime target for surveillance by the factory's Family Planning Commission. From 1983 to 1990, because of the One-Child Policy, I had to have five abortions on the following dates: September 28, 1984; December 17, 1985; March 20, 1986; May 5, 1989; and December 14, 1990. All the operations were recorded in my medical history. I suffered greatly at the hands of the inhumane One-Child Policy.

In the 1980's, shortly after the implementation of the One-Child Policy in China, there were many severe methods of surveillance and punishment to prevent unplanned pregnancies and above-quota births. My factory's Family Planning Commission used three levels of control: at the factory level, in the factory clinic and on the factory floor. There was a system of collective punishment: if one worker violated the rules, all would be punished. Workers monitored each other. Women of reproductive age accounted for 60% of my factory floor. Colleagues were suspicious and hostile to each other because of the One-Child Policy. Two of my pregnancies were reported by my colleagues to the Family Planning Commission. When discovered, pregnant women would be dragged to undergo forced abortions—there simply was no other choice. We had no dignity as potential child-bearers. By order of the factory's Family Planning Commission, every month during their menstrual period, women had to undress in front of the birth planning doctor for examination. If anyone skipped the examination, she would be forced to take a pregnancy test at the hospital. We were allowed to collect a salary only after it was confirmed that we were not pregnant.

The day of my fifth and last abortion, December 14, 1990, was the saddest of my life. Because I was unable to prove that I wasn't pregnant within the 10-15 day time period, the birth planning doctor in the factory clinic found out about my pregnancy. That day, officials from the factory Family Planning Commission drove to the City Police Hospital and forced me to have an abortion in the Birth Planning Department. It was my first operation in that hospital. All my previous abortions happened in the Central City Hospital. I didn't know what the officials in my factory told the doctors. After the abortion, the doctors—without my knowledge—implanted a metal IUD in my uterus. When I learned of the procedure, I protested that I had a kidney disease and could not keep the IUD, but they completely ignored me. The doctors just gave the bill to my husband and told him to pay. While my husband argued with the doctors, I was recovering in a hospital bed. When I left the operating room, still weak, I couldn't find my husband. I was told that he had been arrested. I collapsed crying from the physical toll of the two operations and the emotional shock. A kind nurse tried to comfort me somewhat, but she was shooed away by a man who also threatened to have me arrested by the police. By this time, the Family Planning officials who dragged me to the hospital were nowhere to be found. I felt alone, sick and weak. Afterwards, I learned that my husband had been sentenced to criminal detention without a trial for violating and obstructing the One-Child Policy, disturbing the normal operations of a hospital, and disturbing social peace. My husband was released 15 days later. I was in great pain from the metallic IUD and the weakness of the abortion and almost didn't want to live. The arrest of my husband deprived me of the care of my family. My young son didn't know what was happening and kept crying for his father. I didn't know what to do and could only hold my son and cry with him. Even now, when I think of all this, my heart shudders and the pain throbs.

Those painful 15 days of separation became the catalyst of my eventually failed marriage. My body suffered great damage from all the forced abortions. I gradually grew afraid of family life with my husband. I tried to find excuses to refuse any intimacy demands from my husband. I grew to hate him after the IUD was inserted because I blamed my suffering on his unwillingness to be surgically sterilized. He had known of my kidney disease but would not make any sacrifice for me. I felt no love from him. After the fifth abortion and the IUD insertion, my factory also gave me a "serious administrative warning" and fined me six months' wages. Afterwards, I had to go to the factory clinic every month for exams to make certain that I had not privately taken out the IUD or become pregnant. I carried this IUD in my body for over a decade before I came to America.

My husband's detention accelerated the demise of my marriage. He was suspended from his job and censored, then lost his job in 1991. Our family immediately sank into financial difficulties. We argued frequently. I was laid off at the end of 1995. As I was still considered of reproductive age, the Family Planning Commission of my neighborhood committee took up the job of monitoring me. In early 1997, I spent 40 days taking care of my terminally ill mother and missed the monthly pregnancy check. Agents from the Family Planning Commission waited at my home to drag me to the exam. When they pushed me to the ground, I fell and hurt my neck vertebrae. My spirit completely collapsed after this. I attempted suicide but was stopped by my family from jumping. With the help of old friends, in 1999, I escaped the country that humiliated and destroyed me, and came to the free soil of America.

My husband came to the U.S. a year later. We were unable to mend our past grievances, and divorced in 2001. I became extremely depressed after the divorce, but at the suggestion of my friends I started attending church, where I felt the warmth of Christ's family. The Lord Jesus led me to give up the hatred in my heart, bit by bit. In 2009, my neck injury flared up again. I reunited with my husband when he came to care for me, and we joined together again after I was baptized last year. Now we live in the great family of Christ, in the free land of America. I feel happiness but know that back in China, there are millions of women who are suffering like I did. Every day, thousands of young lives are being destroyed. I beg everyone to save them and wish everyone to join me in a prayer for them. Let the love of our Heavenly Father, the grace of Jesus Christ and the Holy Spirit fill their hearts and release them from the hellish suffering. In the name of our Lord Jesus Christ, amen.

Mr. SMITH. Thank you very much as well for your very courageous testimony and for the reconciliation and peace you have found with God. Unfortunately, that peace evades a huge majority of women in China, and the victims' toll obviously continues by the hour, not just by the day.

I would like to ask our three additional and very distinguished witnesses if they would present their testimony, beginning first with Dr. Valerie Hudson, who is a professor of political science at Brigham Young University, having previously taught at Northwestern and Rutgers.

Her research includes foreign policy analysis, maturity studies, gender and international relations, and methodology. She is the author or editor of several books and coauthored "Bare Branches: The Security Implications of Asia's Surplus Male Population."

Dr. Hudson was named to the list of Foreign Policy Magazine's top 100 global thinkers for 2009, and Dr. Hudson is one of the principal investigators of WomenStats Project, which includes the largest compilation of data on the status of women in the world today.

We will then hear from Ms. Chai Ling, who is the founder of All Girls Allowed, an organization dedicated to restoring life, value and dignity to girls and mothers, and revealing the injustice of China's one-child-per-couple policy.

Ms. Chai Ling has established the Jenzabar Foundation and serves on its board of directors. The foundation supports the most inspirational and influential humanitarian efforts of students through grant opportunities. We all remember her as the key student leader in the 1989 Tiananmen Square movement. She was one of the most wanted by the Chinese dictatorship. She was subsequently named Glamour Magazine's Woman of the Year and nominated twice for the Nobel Peace Prize, and has just published a very incisive book that I hope members will read, as well as the general public.

Finally, we will hear from Ms. Reggie Littlejohn, the president and founder of Women's Rights Without Frontiers, an international coalition that opposes forced abortion, gendercide and sex slavery in China. She has legally represented Chinese refugees in their political asylum cases in the United States. Ms. Littlejohn has briefed the White House, testified before the European and British Parliaments as well as Congress on China's one-child-per-couple policy.

She serves as an expert on the policy for the China AIDS Foundation and Human Rights Without Frontiers. She has issued several groundbreaking reports about the incalculable suffering caused by coercive enforcement of the one-child policy, including a report that she releases today.

Dr. Hudson, please proceed.

STATEMENT OF VALERIE HUDSON, PH.D, PROFESSOR, DEPARTMENT OF POLITICAL SCIENCE, BRIGHAM YOUNG UNIVERSITY

Ms. HUDSON. Mr. Chairman, I will summarize my remarks and ask that my complete written statement be included in the record.

Mr. SMITH. Without objection, so ordered.

Ms. HUDSON. Mr. Chairman, Mr. Fortenberry and other members of the subcommittee, I am grateful that you are holding this hearing. I think this is a crucially important topic and one that should receive greater attention from U.S. policymakers. So I applaud your efforts in this regard.

I have been very moved by the two testimonies that have preceded mine, and I feel honored to sit next to Reggie Littlejohn and Chai Ling, knowing of their great efforts in this area.

China's one-child policy, the policy was first announced in 1978, that was 33 years ago, and Chinese authorities claim it has prevented approximately 400 million births from 1979 to 2011. While the official position of the Chinese Government is that the policy will remain in place until at least 2016, there are rumors that fines and punishments for having a second child for those couples who are not entitled to a second child may in the future no longer be enforced. We will see.

Nevertheless, it is apparent that the Chinese Government may be rethinking the wisdom of the one-child policy in light of current national security concerns. As a security studies specialist, my remarks will focus on the effects of China's one-child policy on the national security of that nation. My argument will be that the one-child policy has not enhanced China's security, but demonstrably weakened it.

As Nick Eberstadt has famously phrased it, what are the consequences for a society that has chosen to become simultaneously both more gray and more male, for that is indisputably what the Chinese Government has chosen by implementing the one-child policy.

The ratio of elderly persons to current workers is plummeting from 5.4 in 2009 to a projected 2.5 in 2030 and 1.6 in 2050, according to CSIS, at the same time that the birth sex ratio has risen officially to over 118 boy babies born for every 100 girl babies in China today, and may, in fact, be as high as 122 or more. We know indeed that in certain areas of China, the birth sex ratio is approaching 140 boy babies for every 100 girl babies. It is time to ask whether the one-child policy has undermined China's ability to sustain itself as a stable and prospering society.

Now, I am sure you are aware that some have argued that the altered sex ratios we have seen are merely an artifact of underreporting of girls, while others have suggested that factors like hepatitis B antigens are playing a role. However, I believe these views are either naive or erroneous. I think the two testimonies that we have already heard tell us something about what is going on, especially as related to the sex of fetuses.

I think it is also interesting, for example, to note the experience of the municipality of Shenzhen in southern China. Alarmed at their rising birth sex ratio, which reached 118 9 years ago, local officials instituted a strict crackdown on black market ultrasound clinics to detect the presence of female fetuses. Offering 200 yuan for tips as to where these clinics could be found, officials then vigorously prosecuted owners of the machines and technicians using them with prison terms affixed. Two years later, the birth sex ratio had fallen to 108, near normal.

So I think it is fair to say that accounts such as these provide support for the thesis that the modern gender imbalance in China is largely man-made. Girls are being culled from the population, rather through prenatal sex identification and female sex selective abortion, or through relative neglect compared to male offspring in early childhood, or through desperate life circumstances that might result in suicide, as the chairman has noted. The gender imbalance in Asia is primarily the result of son preference and the profound devaluation of female life.

Now, the other face of the coin for the missing daughters of China are the excess sons of China. For every daughter culled from the population, a son will become surplus, or, in colloquial Chinese, a bare branch on the family tree. Our own estimates were that by 2020, the number of young adult bare branches would number in excess of 30 million. As noted by the chairman, the Chinese Government's estimates are between 40-, and now I have heard 50 million, in 2020, looking at close to 1 in 5 young adult Chinese men.

No society has ever had to cope with the sheer numbers being produced by the Chinese one-child policy of bare branches. And the percentage of boys that are surplus within their population increases in lockstep according to the year in which they were born. That is, there is a higher percentage of surplus sons in the 1986 birth population than there was in 1985, and more in 1987 than 1986, and so forth and so on. That is, the birth sex ratio has continued to climb despite efforts by the Chinese Government.

It is important to understand which young men become the bare branches who will have little chance of marrying in their society and establishing a family. Well-off young men with education, skills, money, looks or some combination thereof will marry. It is the young men without advantages, those who are poor, unskilled, illiterate, who will find themselves without the ability to form families. The men at these lower socioeconomic levels already feel disenfranchised from established society. Their inability to form a family will deepen their aggrievement with the existing social order.

The foremost repercussions that we have found in our study are increased societal instability marked by increases in crime, violent crime, crimes against women, substance abuse, and, as noted by the chairman, the formation of gangs that are involved in profiting from all of these behaviors. Unattached young adult males are several times more likely to engage in these types of behavior than attached young adult males. And they tend to congregate, and when they do, their behavior as a group is more antisocial than the behavior of each individual would be by himself.

These empirical findings toll not just for China, but across nationally. We have detailed numerous historical cases in both China, in India and in other lands in Asia where abnormal sex ratios lead to domestic instability and conflict between national and regionally based coalitions of bare branches.

What I would like now to look at is the broader ramifications of these trends. I suggest that when we step back and take a larger perspective, when we look at the phenomenon of global aging, as well as China's aging, the likely economic effect of aging, and we combine that with the analysis of the effects of abnormal sex ratios on a society, the synergistic effects of these trends are likely to be quite dangerous for the Chinese Government.

In addition to the current economic woes that we are all experiencing, economists predict there will also come an economic slowdown in the coming decades due to the aging of the most advanced economies. This global slow down is likely to amplify the economic storm clouds already looming for China. A society with a masculinized young adult population such as China's is likely to respond to their coming significant economic hardship, which makes the pale effects of the current economic recession on China very dilute by comparison. I believe that China is likely to respond—this society will likely respond with severe domestic instability and crime.

The Chinese regime will be hard-pressed to maintain its usual control over society as a result and will likely become more authoritarian as time goes on to meet this internal security challenge.

It may well be that the Chinese Government could play upon nationalist themes to maintain power in the context of an aging yet more masculine society experiencing a profound economic slowdown. The government could use, say, anti-Japanese or anti-Taiwan independence themes to galvanize not only the elderly generation, but, more importantly, the young adult generation which is highly masculinized.

Masculine societies are very susceptible to political campaigns stressing national pride vis-à-vis a competing nation. But masculine societies are a double-edged sword in this also, for if the government is perceived as weak or as unsuccessful in these contests of national pride, it will be very vulnerable to internal dissension that would bring a stronger government to power.

In sum then, from all that we have analyzed to this point, the abnormal sex ratios of China as well as its increased aging, both due to the one-child policy, does not bode well for its future. Even if the sex ratios were somehow magically rectified today, which they certainly will not be, young adult sex ratios in China will result in a significant percentage of bare branches for at least the next 30 years. And economists tell us it is around the year 2020 that China will enter a crucial period.

In 2020, China will still be adding workers to its population before the downturn in its working population hits around 2030, while the richest nations of the world fade from global dominion due to aging. A lingering economic slowdown plus the opportunities afforded by the fading of the West and Japan, will create a unique crucible for a possible dramatic change in China's security situation.

Now, while it is true that the demographic die has been cast for the next few decades in China, it is also true that relinquishing the one-child policy would positively affect China's future prospects for stability, security and prosperity. That the Chinese Government is now pondering whether to turn to a de facto two-child policy is an interesting development, indicating that the government now sees more clearly the security issues the one-child policy has raised.

Even so, steering the ship of culture to a new heading will be a very difficult undertaking. In experiments performed by the government in selected areas, institution of a two-child policy did not change the fertility rate, and it did not change the sex ratio of the births.

On the basis of these experimental findings, we are now forced to wonder whether the one-child policy will have significant cultural effects and demographic effects that will long outlast the policy itself. If that is the case, that will be truly a tragedy for China.

Thank you very much.

[The prepared statement of Ms. Hudson follows:]

September 20, 2011

Testimony before the Subcommittee on Africa, Global Health, and Human Rights of the House Foreign Affairs Committee
Subcommittee meeting held on 22 September 2011

Valerie M. Hudson
Professor, Political Science
Brigham Young University
Valerie_hudson@byu.edu

Thank you for the opportunity to testify before this subcommittee on the topic of China's One-Child Policy. The policy was first announced in 1978—33 years ago—and Chinese authorities claim it has prevented approximately 400 million births from 1979 to 2011. While the official position of the Chinese government is that the policy will remain in place until at least 2015, there are rumors that fines and punishments for having a second child (for those couples who are not entitled to a second child) may no longer be enforced. It is apparent that the Chinese government is re-thinking the wisdom of the One-Child Policy in light of current national security concerns.

As a Security Studies specialist, my remarks will focus on the effects China's One-Child policy has had on the national security of that nation. My argument will be that the One-Child policy has not enhanced China's security, but demonstrably weakened it. As Nick Eberstadt famously phrased it, what are the consequences for a society that has chosen to become, simultaneously, both more gray and more male? For that is indisputably what the Chinese government has chosen by implementing the One-Child Policy. The ratio of elderly persons to current workers is plummeting (from 5.4 in 2009 to a projected 2.5 in 2030 and 1.6 in 2050, according to CSIS), at the same time that the birth sex ratio has risen (officially) to over 118 boy babies born for every 100 girls babies, and may in fact be as high as 122 or more. Indeed, certain areas of China are approaching a ratio of 140.

It is time to ask whether the One-Child Policy has undermined China's ability to sustain itself as a stable and a prospering society.

Introduction

The most frequently discussed transnational demographic change of the twenty-first century is that of global aging. Many developed nations are aging, and quite a few have birth rates that are at subreplacement levels. Researchers and policymakers alike have become intensely interested in understanding the social, economic, and security consequences of that vast demographic shift among the most powerful nations in the international system.

But in Asia there is a second unprecedented demographic alteration taking place: over the last twenty years, birth sex ratios have become increasing skewed in favor of males. This phenomenon can be found in nations such as China, India, Pakistan, Bangladesh, Nepal, Taiwan, and South Korea. Overall, there are at least 90 million missing women in Asia, and over 10% of young adult men in these nations will be hard pressed to form traditional families of their own. And for China, a rising power, *both* demographic shifts are at work—China is not only one of the "aging" countries, it is also the country with the greatest shift in sex ratios. China's last census shows that over 118 male babies are born for every 100 girl babies born, and in reality this ratio is likely higher, closer to 122:100 (normal ratios are 105-107 males born per 100 females born).

In my co-authored book, *Bare Branches: The Security Implications of Asia's Surplus Male Population* (MIT, 2004, with Andrea M. Den Boer), we assert that the increasing skewedness of birth sex ratios in Asia will lead to greater societal instability and crime, with real ramifications for regional and even international security. In this paper, I will re-cap that analysis, as well as adding to it a new and original discussion of the interaction effects between abnormal sex ratios, economic and cultural trends pertinent to China, and global aging, with particular emphasis on consequences for regional and international security.

I. Missing Daughters in China

That there is an abnormal deficit of females in Asia can be fairly readily confirmed through standard demographic analysis. There are established ranges for normal variation in overall population sex ratios, as well as early childhood and birth sex ratios. These ratios are adjusted for country-specific circumstances such as, for example, maternal mortality rates and infant mortality rates. Using official census data, it is then a relatively straightforward task to determine if there are fewer women than could reasonably be expected in a given population. Of course, there are perturbing variables: for example, many of the Gulf States have very abnormal sex ratios favoring males, but this is due to the high number of guest workers, predominantly male, that labor in the oil economies of these states. Once these types of factors have been taken into account, we find that a deficit of females in Asia is a real phenomenon.

To see the scale of the deficit, some comparisons are in order. If we examine overall population sex ratios, the ratio for, say, Latin America is 99.5 males per 100 females (using 2000 figures)—the corresponding figure for Asia is 106 males per 100 females. But one must also keep in mind the sheer size of the populations of Asia: India and China alone comprise about 40% of the world's population. Thus, the overall sex ratio of the world is 104.1, despite the fact that the ratios for the rest of the world (excluding Oceania) range from 103.1 (Europe) to 99.5 (Africa).[1]

Birth sex ratios in several Asian countries are also outside of the established norm of 105-107 boy babies born for every 100 girl babies. The Indian government's estimate of its birth sex ratio is approximately 113 boy babies born for every 100 girl babies, with some locales noting ratios of 156 and higher. The Chinese government states that its birth sex ratio is slightly over 118 (2010 Census results), though some Chinese scholars have gone on record as stating the birth sex ratio is at least 121-122. Again, in some locations, the ratio is higher: the island of

---

[1] Population Division of the Department of Economics and Social Affairs of the United Nations Secretariat, *World Population Progress: The 2002 Revision* and *World Urbanization Prospects: The 2001 Revision,* http://esa.un.org/unpp/

Hainan's birth sex ratio is 135 (in 2000). Other countries of concern include Pakistan, Bangladesh, Nepal, Bhutan, Taiwan, Afghanistan, and South Korea. No data is available for North Korea.[2]

Another indicator of gender imbalance is early childhood mortality. Boys typically have a higher early childhood mortality rate, which virtually cancels out their birth sex ratio numerical advantage by age 5. The reasons for this higher mortality include sex-linked genetic mutations, such as hemophilia, as well as higher death rates for boys from common childhood diseases, such as dysentery. However, in some of the Asian nations just mentioned, including China, early childhood mortality rates for girls are actually higher than those for boys.[3] Furthermore, orphanage populations are predominantly female in these nations.

Other statistics also factor into the observed gender imbalance. In the West, for example, male suicides far outnumber female suicides. But in countries with deficits of women, female suicides outnumber male suicides. In fact, approximately 55% of all female suicides in the world are Chinese women of childbearing age.[4]

What forces drive the deficit of females in Asian nations such as China? How do we account for the disappearance of so many women from these populations—estimated conservatively at over 90 million missing women in seven Asian countries alone?

Some scholars assert that there may be a physical cause at work preventing female births, such as the disease hepatitis B, antigens of which have been associated with higher birth sex ratios.[5] This has been disproved as a significant contributing factor. Rather, it is worth considering the following experience of the municipality of Shenzen in southern China. Alarmed at their rising birth sex ratio, which reached 118 in 2002, local officials instituted a strict crackdown on black market ultrasound clinics. Offering 200 yuan for tips as to where these clinics could be found, officials then vigorously prosecuted owners of the machines and technicians using them, with prison terms affixed. By 2004—that is, in just two years--the birth sex ratio had dropped to 108.[6]

It is fair to say that accounts such as these provide support for the thesis that the modern gender imbalance in Asia, as with historical gender imbalances in Asia and elsewhere, is largely a man-made phenomenon. Girls are being culled from the population, whether through prenatal sex identification and female sex selective abortion, or through relative neglect compared to male offspring in early childhood

---

[2] See Table 2.3 on p. 60 of Valerie M. Hudson and Andrea M. Den Boer, *Bare Branches: The Security Implications of Asia's Surplus Male Population*, Camrbridge: MIT Press, 2005.

[3] *Ibid, pp. 176-77.*

[4] Christopher J.L. Murray and Alan D. Lopez (eds.), *The Global Burden of Disease: A Comprehensive Assessment of Mortality and Disability from Diseases, Injuries, and Risk Factors in 1990 and Projected to 2020*, Cambridge, Mass: Harvard University Press, 1996, p. 448 and Elisabeth Rosenthal, "Women's Suicides Reveal Rural China's Bitter Roots," *New York Times*, January 24, 1999, sec. 1, p. 1.

[5] Oster, Emily, "Hepatitis B and the Case of the Missing Women," *Journal of Political Economy*, 113, no. 6 (December 2005): 1163-1216.

[6] *People's Daily Online*, 'Shenzhen's Newborn Sex Ratio More Balanced', 15 April 2005, http://english.people.com.cn/200504/15/eng20050415_181218.html.

(including abandonment), or through desperate life circumstances that might result in suicide. The gender imbalance in Asia is primarily the result of son preference and the profound devaluation of female life.

One could justifiably suggest that this value ordering is not confined to Asia; why, then, is the deficit of women found almost exclusively there? This question can only be approached through a multifactorial cultural analysis, which we will not detail in this short statement. Suffice it to say that one must examine variables such as religious prohibition or sanction of the practice, traditions of patrilocality and old age security obtained through male offspring, issues of dowry, hypergyny, and caste purity in India, as well as the effect of interventions such as the one-child policy in China. Other factors to consider include the web of incentives, disincentives, and capabilities surrounding the issue of prenatal sex determination technology. The 2010 census in China provides the most recent comprehensive statistics for China's population, but only preliminary results have been released thus far. According to the census the overall sex ratio in China was 105.2, far above the 98-99 that is normal. The birth sex ratio for China in 2010 was over 118. We have more detailed figures from the 2000 census. Of the 14 million births from November 1999 to November 2000, 7.6 million were male and only 6.5 million were female, resulting in a birth sex ratio of 116.9.[7] China's birth sex ratio has been increasing for the past twenty years: in 1981, shortly after the introduction of China's one-child policy designed to slow population growth, the sex ratio at birth was 108.5. Birth sex ratios varied from province to province, with only two provinces at or near the expected sex ratio of 105.0 (Tibet and Xinjiang) and some provinces exhibiting sex ratios as high as 128.2 (Hubei), 130.3, (Guangdong), and 135.6 (Hainan). We look forward to the release of these types of detailed figures from the 2010 Census in the near future.

Childhood sex ratios are similarly high: sex ratios for children ages 1-4 have increased from 107.0 in 1982 to 120.8 in 2000.[8] Early childhood sex ratios vary throughout China according to the 2000 census, with only one province (Tibet) exhibiting a sex ratio at or below a ratio of 105.0, and ten provinces exhibiting sex ratios above China's average (with ratios as high as 135.7 in Hainan, 136.4 in Henan and 136.8 in Jiangxi).[9] Whereas childhood sex ratios typically fall below that of the birth sex ratio due to higher male infant and early childhood mortality patterns, some of China's childhood sex ratios are actually higher than birth sex ratios, indicating the presence of discriminatory practices against female infants and children.

---

[7] Guowuyuan renkou pucha bangongshi, *Zhongguo 2000 nian renkou pucha ziliao,* Volume 1, Table 1-12. Preliminary 2010 results:
http://af.reuters.com/article/metalsNews/idAFL3E7FS1Z920110428?sp=true
[8] China, Population Census Office, The 1982 Population Census of China; China, State Statistical Bureau; and *Guowuyuan renkou pucha bangongshi, Zhongguo 2000 nian renkou pucha ziliao,* Volume 1, Table 1-7.
[9] *Guowuyuan renkou pucha bangongshi, Zhongguo 2000 nian renkou pucha ziliao,* Volume 1, Table 1-7.

The result of the high sex ratios at birth, coupled with differential infant and childhood mortality patterns in China is that there are 40.6 million women missing from the population (in 2000; we still await the results for 2010). Furthermore, women are not missing in older cohorts: missing women are found in young cohorts of the population, and the younger the cohort, the greater the proportion and number of missing women. This is a demographic phenomenon whose effects are only now beginning to be felt in the larger society, but these effects will grow over time with each passing year.

II. Security Implications of Rising Numbers of Bare Branches in China

The other face of the coin from the missing daughters of China, are the excess sons of China. For every daughter culled from the population, a son will become "surplus"—or in colloquial Chinese, a "bare branch" on the family tree. Our estimates are that by the year 2020, young adult bare branches (ages 15-34) will number approximately 23-25 million in China alone, which constitutes 13% of this young adult male population. No society has ever had to cope with these numbers of bare branches before. The boys born in 1985, when Chinese birth sex ratios originally began to rise significantly, are turning 21 this year, and the percentage of boys that are surplus increases in lock-step according to the year in which they were born. That is, there is a higher percentage of surplus sons in the 1986 birth population than in 1985, and in 1987 than 1986, and so forth.

It is important to understand which young men become the bare branches who will have little chance of marrying and establishing a family, Well-off young men with education, skills, money, looks, or some combination thereof, will marry. It is the young men without advantages--those who are poor, unskilled, illiterate-- who will find themselves without the ability to form families. The men at these lower socio-economic levels already feel disenfranchised from established society; their inability to form a family deepens their aggrievement with the existing social order.

In every human society, one important task is to transition young adult males who have little stake in a social order based on law--and who would prefer a social order based on physical force wherein they would possess a natural advantage--to the position of having a meaningful stake in society. That is typically accomplished through marriage and the birth of children, marking the passage from bachelorhood to head of household status. One of the few "laws" in sociology is that male criminal behavior drops significantly upon marriage or serious commitment. In societies where that passage is non-voluntarily delayed for a majority of men, as in some Middle Eastern countries, or where that transition cannot occur for a sizeable percentage of young men, as in China and India, there will be negative social repercussions. By 2020, at least 13% of young adult males in China will not be making that transition.

The foremost repercussions will be an increase in societal instability, marked by increases in crime, violent crime, crimes against women, vice, substance abuse,

and the formation of gangs involved in all of these antisocial behaviors.[10]
Unattached young adult males are several times more likely to engage in these types
of behaviors than attached young adult males. Furthermore, unattached young
adult males tend to congregate, and when they do, their behavior as a group is more
antisocial than the behavior of each individual would be by himself. These empirical
findings hold cross-nationally: young adult males, especially unattached young adult
males, monopolize violence in every human society.

In addition to these types of antisocial behavior, sometimes bare branch
gangs coalesce into small armies, which may further coalesce into larger forces that
challenge the authority of the government in their area. One such example is the
Nien Rebellion in China in the mid-1800's, which opposed the imperial government
in the north at the same time that another movement, the Taiping, was active in the
south.[11] The Nien originated in the Huai-pei area of China around 1851, as it was
known at the time, where because of severe natural and man-made disasters,
families turned to female infanticide to such a degree that the sex ratio was
approximately 129. Young men, mostly bare branches, coalesced into smuggling
gangs. Over time, the gangs merged, and as their forces grew larger, so did their
aspirations. A county magistrate in Nien territory concluded that three categories of
men were creating the unrest--bare branches, smugglers, and bandits--and that the
overlap between the three groups was very great. By 1862, the Nien were in control
of territory containing almost six million people. It took the imperial army until
1868 to finally crush the rebellion.

We have detailed other historical cases in both China and India where
abnormal sex ratios led to domestic instability and conflict between national and
regionally-based coalitions of bare branches.[12] Because of space constraints, I wish
to turn to a non-Asian case--that of medieval Portugal--to explore international
security ramifications of abnormal sex ratios.

Due to an interesting confluence of factors, son preference was enacted in
medieval Portugal, leading to an adult sex ratio of 112, with youth ratio somewhat
higher. During this time, lower class Portuguese bare branches would throw in their
lot with bare branch sons of landed nobility to produce an array of small armies
whose chief means of support was plunder and banditry. During periods of political
upheaval, bands of bare branches, backed by force of arms, supported challengers to
the regime who promised to redistribute the country's wealth. Alternatively, the
regime would send bare branches on foreign adventures of conquest and
colonization. One historical anthropologist, James Boone, cites the case of João I, the
illegitimate half-brother of the Portuguese monarch, who seized the throne after the
latter-s death with the help of bare branch armies (Boone calls them "cadet bands").
When João I discovered that these bands, through piracy and robbery, were
beginning to threaten his own rule, he obtained Papal consent to launch the

---

[10] Please see discussion pp. 192-200 in Valerie M. Hudson and Andrea M. Den Boer, *op cit.*, for a
wide-ranging literature review on the phenomena explored here.

[11] This account draws upon Elizabeth Perry, *Rebels and Revolutionaries in North China, 1845-1945,*
Stanford, Calif: Stanford University Press, 1980.

[12] See pp. 214-227 in Hudson and Den Boer, *op cit.*

Reconquista—Portugal's military campaign along the North African coast. Boone remarks, "It was above all *the cadets*, who lacked land and other sources of revenue within the country who desired war, which would permit them to acceded to a situation of social and material independence."[13] Another historian notes, "It is obvious that it was the bands of 'youths' excluded by so many social prohibitions from the main body of settled men, fathers of families and heads of houses, with their prolonged spells of turbulent behavior making them an unstable fringe of society, who created and sustained the crusades."[14] By the mid-sixteenth century, nearly 25% of adult noble males had died in the crusades, which did serve to reduce the number of bare branches in Portuguese society—albeit while simultaneously initiating interstate war.

III. Government Response in China

Governments do recognize the growing threat from bare branch collectives. Historical commentaries from China, India, and other nations make reference to bare branches as a source of instability. The problem for these governments is how to meet this internal threat. The focus of most governmental policies becomes lowering the number of bare branches. Several strategies have been used historically to this end: encouragement of outmigration, colonization of frontier areas, initiation of large scale public works projects, easing inmigration of women, and so forth. We do see some of these strategies in use already in China, such as the increasing migration of Chinese, especially young adult males, to the Russian Far East and other areas, expansion of settlement efforts in Xinjiang, erection of the Three Gorges Dam and immense canal projects, and a more-or-less blind eye to cross-border chattel markets in women from North Korea, Laos, Vietnam, Myanmar and other nations. But arguably China has not yet faced the real future of this possible threat. As noted previously, the boys born in 1985 are 19 turning 21 this year, and with each passing year, both the sheer number and the proportion of bare branches in China (and India, and Pakistan, and Taiwan, and several other surrounding nations) will grow immensely.

In our survey of the historical literature, we also found two other troubling trends. Governments facing appreciable numbers of bare branches would move toward greater authoritarianism to counter the instability created. And in a few cases, it became clear that the government coopted bare branches into the military to lower their level of resentment, but then found it necessary to send those armies away on distant adventures for fear of the ramifications of keeping these bloated armies close to population centers and seats of power. Arming bare branches, and training them in military tactics, only amplified the threat they posed to the government. In a sense, then, the prospects for both democracy and peace were diminished by the creation of large numbers of bare branches in society.

---

[13] James Boone, "Noble Family Structure and Expansionist Warfare in the Late Middle Ages," in Rada Dyson-Hudson and Michael A, Little (eds.), *Rethinking Human Adaptation: Biological and Cultural Models*, Boulder, Colo: Westview Press, 1980, p. 94.

[14] Boone, *ibid*, p. 94.

As security analysts contemplate the future of conflicts such as Jammu and Kashmir, and the Taiwan Strait, it is worthwhile to keep in mind that the calculus of deterrence may be altered by the presence of large numbers of bare branches in the affected countries over the next 2-3 decades. Though abnormal sex ratios are certainly no necessary condition for any conflict or war (for example, the sex ratio of Rwanda in 1994 was normal), predispositions to conflict may be aggravated by the existence of a large surplus of young adult males in one's society. The reason for this is that when the domestic instability caused by bare branch collectives evolves into a more direct threat to government control of society, the government will see the internal threat from bare branches as more threatening than traditional external threats. We have seen how, in the case of medieval Portugal, interstate war was initiated by the Portuguese monarch in order to save his own rule from the threat posed by bare branch collectives. That those wars were long and bloody turned out to be the very reason they were initiated: to send bare branches away from the country and to cause high levels of attrition among them.

In a move that can only be applauded, on July 15, 2004 the Chinese government announced a new, nationwide initiative to normalize the birth sex ratio by the year 2010. (The government later changed the target year to 2016.) This is to be accomplished by offering financial incentives to parents of daughters, including small old age pensions. In December 2004, the Chinese government also proposed the criminalization of sex selective abortion, though that measure was later dropped. Some provinces have banned abortion beyond 14-16 weeks, which is before sex can be identified through ultrasound. Others have required that a panel of three doctors approve the abortion of a female fetus. Still others have offered large rewards for turning in information relating to "black market" ultrasound clinics. There is also talk of loosening the one-child policy to become a two-child policy in the next 5-10 years. However, it is also fair to say that the horse has left the barn for at least the next twenty years: the alterations in the birth sex ratios of 1985-2010 cannot now be undone for China (or any of the other nations with abnormal sex ratios). Asia, and possibly the world, will live with the results of this contempt for daughters for many years to come.

Furthermore, scientists are perfecting a blood test that will allow non-invasive identification of the sex of fetuses at seven weeks' gestation through a simple blood test. The pace of technology will make it even easier to discard unwanted female fetuses in the very near future.[15]

IV. Interaction Effects in China: Economic, Cultural, and Demographic Factors

We cannot look at China's abnormal sex ratios in a vacuum. There are other factors of an economic, cultural, and demographic nature, which must be considered alongside the rise of bare branches in China.

Most of the developed nations of the world, including all of Europe (east and west) and Japan, are aging. China is aging also, due to the one-child policy. The

---

[15] Lindsey Tanner (Associated Press), "Boy or Girl? A Simple Test Raises Ethical Concerns," Deseret News, 9 August 2011, http://www.deseretnews.com/article/700169557/Boy-or-girl-A-simple-test-raises-ethical-concerns.html , accessed 20 September 2011.

2010 Census figures show that the over-60 cohort is now 13% of China's population. China is different from the other aging countries of the world, however, in that it is not yet fully developed, and most of its population is still poor. Robert Stowe England notes that by 2055, China's elderly population will exceed the elderly population of all of North America, Europe, and Japan combined.[16] Furthermore, the working age population of China is expected to peak in 2025, and begin to decline thereafter.

Aging will have numerous economic effects, which are already beginning to be felt in Europe and Japan. Declining working-age populations are a drag on economic growth. Consumption patterns between workers and the elderly are quite different, also, with the elderly consuming much less than workers (especially in the area of durable goods), except in the area of health care. According to Nyce and Schieber, to maintain current standard of living in countries with a shrinking population, these nations will have to import more or produce more, but if consumer spending falls also, there are likely to be lay-offs and rising unemployment as well.[17] Aging societies also have significantly lower savings rates, as the elderly must divest themselves of their assets to maintain their standard of living in a context of rising health care costs. As a result, capital investment both at home and abroad may be compromised. Businesses may experience a lower return on investment in their homeland, but increasing investment abroad may lead to a net capital outflow, which may result in the weakening of the currencies of aging societies. Nyce and Schieber also note that if aging brings with it higher pension costs, this will lead to fewer low income jobs, wage depression, slowing economic growth and job creation, declining interest from foreign investors, lower entrepreneurship, and higher budget deficits.[18]

The CSIS Commission on Global Aging also suggests that aging societies will shift their spending priorities, with a lower priority now placed on infrastructure, defense, and education. Labor force declines also translate into lower tax revenues for governments, and if these governments are tempted by deficit financing, global financial stability may be compromised. The CSIS Commission feels that there may be a shift in global economic, political, and perhaps even military power away from aging societies. The lack of savings may cause interest rates to rise globally, perhaps even prompting a global recession.[19]

Interestingly, this Commission also predicts that the position of China could be quite crucial in the context of global aging. China has increasingly become a repository for pension wealth from developed countries, and the Commission wonders if this means that China can continue its high economic growth even in the

---

[16] Robert Stowe England, *The Demographic Challenge to China's Economic Prospects*, CSIS Report, Westport, Conn: Praeger, 2005, p. 1.

[17] Steven A. Nyce and Sylvester J. Schieber, *The Economic Implications of Aging Societies*, New York: Cambridge University Press, 2005, p. 166.

[18] Nyce and Scheiber, *op cit.*, pp. 226-9, 237.

[19] *Meeting the Challenges of Global Aging*, CSIS Commission on Global Aging, Washington, DC: CSIS Press, 2002.

context of its own aging, or whether China was begin to act in a more mercantilist fashion, which might lead to a new global depression.[20]

Nyce and Schieber remind us that economic slowdowns are accompanied by significant domestic unrest.[21] Indeed, since China's accession to the WTO, unemployment rates have risen significantly: true unemployment in China may be 12-20%.[22] This has been accompanied by an explosion of labor unrest in China. Crime, too, has increased alarmingly in China, which many attribute to the breakdown of the *hukou* system of residence registration and the resulting tidal wave of "floaters" migrating to the metropoles. Some estimates state that approximately 10% of the population of China are among the "floating population," and that the floating population is a grave internal security risk.[23] The floating population is overwhelmingly young adult, and predominantly male.[24] Nicholas Kristof, the noted correspondent, writes that, "Wildcat protests, some violent and involving thousands of people, have been exploding around the country. By the Chinese government's own count, there are now more than 200 protests a day, prompted by everything from layoffs to governmental seizures of land. The protests may grow if, as seems likely, China's economic model appears less miraculous in the years ahead."[25] Gang activity, a hallmark of bare branch economic resistance to societal marginalization, has also grown explosively in recent years.

When we look at global aging, China's aging, and the likely economic effects of aging and combine that with an analysis of the effects of abnormal sex ratios on a society, the synergistic effects are likely to be quite dangerous for the Chinese government. In addition to current global economic woes, there will also come an inevitable economic slowdown primarily due to aging in the most advanced economies. This global slowdown is likely to amplify the economic storm clouds already looming for China. A society with a masculinized young adult population, such as China's, is likely to respond to significant economic hardship with severe domestic instability and crime. The Chinese regime will be hard-pressed to maintain its usual control over society as a result, and will likely become more authoritarian as time goes on to meet this internal security challenge.

The question for the government will be, how can it attract the allegiance of its bare branches, and channel them towards less internally destructive deeds? One temptation may be to play the card of nationalism, and it is here that we must examine some elements of Chinese culture for clues to the future.

It has often been noted by psychologists that youth take their understanding of their nation and its place in the world from the experiences of their forebears,

---

[20] CSIS Commission, *ibid.*, p. 52.

[21] Nyce and Schieber, *op cit.*, p. 179.

[22] England, *op cit.*, p. 66.

[23] Brian Nichiporuk, *The Security Dynamics of Demographic Factors*, MR-1088-WFHF/RF/DLPF/A (RAND, 2000), p. 39.

[24] Hudson and Den Boer, *op cit.*, p. 234.

[25] Nicholas Kristof, "Rumblings from China, *New York Times,* 2 July 2006, A29.

typically the generation of their grandparents.[26] What types of vivid experiences will the grandparents of today's young adults in China tell them about? This generation of forebears would have been born about 1935. They would have lived as young children through the invasion of Japan, which would have left them with deep-seated animosity towards the Japanese. But they would also have seen in their youth the corruption of the Nationalists during the civil war period, and feel a sense of unfulfillment that that regime escaped to Taiwan, preventing the complete unification of China. They would feel a great deal of ambivalence about U.S. support of the regime on Taiwan. At the same time, they would have been starting their careers during the Cultural Revolution, and may have seen their own families, especially their parents, devastated through ideological extremism. They may, in fact, prefer a strong technocratic authoritarian hand to quell social chaos and ensure economic prosperity. This generation, then, is highly nationalistic, anti-Japanese, has strong feelings about the reunification of Taiwan with the mainland, is ambivalent towards the United States, and may be more inclined to respect authoritarian measures to ensure social stability.

It may be that the Chinese government would be able to play upon these themes to maintain power in the context of an aging, more masculine society experiencing a profound economic slowdown. The government could use anti-Japanese, anti-Taiwan independence themes to galvanize not only the elderly generation, but more importantly, the young adult generation. Masculine societies are very susceptible to political campaigns stressing national pride vis a vis a competing nation. But masculine societies are a double-edged sword in this, also, for if the government is perceived as weak or as unsuccessful in these contests of national pride, it will be very vulnerable to internal dissension that would bring a "stronger" government to power.

It is also worth noting that an increasingly masculinized society may also be a society more prone to certain types of disease. It has recently been noted that the surplus young adult males of China provide what epidemiologists call a "bridging population" for transmission of HIV/AIDs into Chinese society.[27] Researchers have found that surplus males engage in riskier sexual behavior (multiple partners, use of prostitutes, non-use of condoms), increased sale of blood, and increased use of illicit drugs. All of these behaviors increase the likelihood of contracting HIV, and since China has only rudimentary screening and care of HIV patients, contraction of HIV infection portends almost inevitable development of full-blown AIDS. China's AIDS problem, only recently acknowledged by the national government, will almost certainly be worsened by its abnormal sex ratios.

---

[26] See, for example, Jason Hart, ""Children and Nationalism in a Palestinian Refugee Camp in Jordan," *Childhood* 9(1): 35-47, 2002' Sharon Stephens, "Childhood and Nationalism," *Childhood* 4(1):5-17.

[27] Joseph D. Tucker, Gail E. Henderson, Tian F. Wang, Ying Y. Huang, William Parish, Sui M. Pan, Xiang S. Chen, Myron S. Cohen, "Surplus Men, Sex Work, and the Spread of HIV in China," *AIDS*, 2005, 19:539-47.

V. Overall Assessment for Security Planners

From all that we have analyzed to this point, the abnormal sex ratios of China do not bode well for its future. Even if sex ratios were rectified today (which they will not be), young adult sex ratios in China will result in a significant percentage of bare branches for the next 30 years. Around the year 2020, China will enter a crucial period. In 2020, China will still be adding workers to its population, while the richest nations of the world fade from global dominion due to aging. A lingering global economic slowdown, plus the opportunities afforded by the fading of the West and Japan, will create a unique crucible for possible dramatic change in China's security situation.

Over time, as the current recession is deepened into a chronic condition by the aging of the richest nations, is likely to create significant unrest and instability in China, all made worse by its abnormal sex ratios. Regionally-based threats to the national government's primacy may arise. Gang-based violence, already worsening, may coagulate into larger threats, as gangs combine to augment their power vis a vis the government. China may be tempted to improve its situation with mercantilist policies, but economists feel this would more likely lead to a prolonged global depression, which would only worsen China's outlook.

Faced with worsening instability at home, and an unsolvable economic decline, China's government may well be tempted to use foreign policy to "ride the tiger" of domestic instability. The twin themes of anti-Japanese feeling and unfulfillment of China's reunification with Taiwan will still be deeply resonant to much of the population of China at that time. In fact, these may be the only themes left that could unite the Chinese population behind the national government. In addition, the government will be searching for contests of national pride involving martial prowess, which will be highly attractive to the bare branch population that will be causing it severe internal problems. The threat from within at this time may be seen by the government as much more pressing than the forces of international deterrence. Might a situation develop where the government sees a way to kill two birds with one stone, seizing a greater share of international power through successful international use of force, while also thinning the ranks of its bare branches through attrition warfare? The perceived alternative may be to see China disintegrate into smaller geographical units, an alternative the Chinese Communist Party is unlikely to ever countenance.

There are also opportunities to the north. The Russian Far East is rapidly depopulating, and is at the same time the site of most of Russia's great mineral and oil wealth. There has been a tremendous influx of Chinese into this area, with the result that over 8% of the population of the Russian Far East is, in fact, Chinese. Bare branches have traditionally been the first colonizers sent abroad, and it may be that Chinese bare branches will play an important role in the Sinification of the Russian Far East. Economic control of these natural resources would place China in a much better position to lighten the economic decline its country faced. But it would also have grave geopolitical consequences for the international community. Would Russia countenance this demographic colonization of the seat of its wealth? Could Russia stop this trend, even if it wanted to do so? What would be the economic consequences for the West?

In conclusion, then, in the next two to three decades, we are likely to see observable security ramifications of the masculinization of China's young adult population, especially when combined with an understanding of the consequences of global aging, the particularities of Chinese nationalism, and the epidemiology of pandemics such as AIDS. Indeed, some of these ramifications are already coming into view. China's contempt for its daughters may lead to a more dangerous world not only for the Chinese themselves, but for everyone.

Conclusion

While it is true that the demographic die has been cast for the next few decades in China, it is also true that relinquishing the One-Child Policy would positively affect China's future prospects for stability, security, and prosperity. That the Chinese government is now pondering whether to turn to a Two-Child policy is an interesting development, indicating that the government now sees more clearly the security issues the One-Child Policy has raised. Even so, steering the ship of culture to a new heading is a very difficult undertaking. In experiments performed by the government in selected areas, institution of a Two-Child Policy did not change the fertility rate. Most families still preferred to have only one child. And son preference did not abate, either. On the basis of these experimental findings, we are now forced to wonder whether the One-Child policy will have significant cultural effects that will long outlast the policy itself. If that is the case, that will truly be a tragedy for China.

Mr. SMITH. Thank you so much for your testimony and for flying from Salt Lake City to be here. I know you are going right back today. We deeply appreciate that inconvenience to your schedule.

Ms. HUDSON. It was an honor to be here.

Mr. SMITH. Thank you so very much, and for the issues you raised that, frankly, have not been raised by many people anywhere, and certainly not with the analysis and the scholarship that you and your colleague have brought to this issue. And I hope the Pentagon, I hope the Commerce Department, the State Department—and I will ask you questions later whether or not they have reacted to any of this, because the way I look at it, they seem to be tone deaf to the information that you have raised. So thank you so very, very much.

I would now like to ask Chai Ling, Ms. Chai, if she would present her testimony.

STATEMENT OF MS. CHAI LING, FOUNDER, ALL GIRLS ALLOWED

Ms. CHAI. Chairman Smith, Congressman Fortenberry and members of the committee, thank you for giving me this opportunity to testify about this massive problem in hope and determination that one day it will come to an end. I am honored to be here with you, with Reggie, and Valerie I just got to know, and the other two distinguished witnesses.

Without, Chairman Smith, your persistent effort to battle on behalf of women and children in China, a hearing in November 2009, and the bold witness of Reggie, I would not be here to be able to continue this work. So thank you. I am very grateful.

As we are here to report and mourn for the loss of 400-plus million lives that have been taken from China since 1980 under China's one-child policy, it only came to full realization recently to me as I was finishing my memoir that three of those babies were mine. And the reason why the one-child policy killed millions of infants and unborn children annually is because it is a one-child-per-couple policy. It is, in effect, an "all the other children must die" policy. That means most married couples are not allowed to have more than one child, and, of course, unmarried women in China are not allowed to have babies at all.

There are 16 million forced and coerced abortions a year in China, but when counting on the numbers of abortion pills sold, possibly close to 23 million. According to the Chinese Government's own statement, more than 70 percent of these women are by those who are unmarried. That means more than 10 million young women suffer this fate every year, up to 27,000 every day, 19 every minute. I want to call your attention to that—to the poster of the young lady who is hiding her face in the IV. In seeing her face, I saw myself many, many years ago.

The tragic equation for millions of unmarried women, especially those too young to wed, is no marriage certificate, no birth permit; no birth permit, no baby.

The first time I became pregnant, I was 18 years old, a sophomore at Peking University. I was terrified and deeply ashamed. All I could think was a scene I saw. A young couple when I first arrived at Peking University was being expelled in front of all of us freshman because she was found to be in love and pregnant. The thought of being taken out of school, which represented life, future, jobs and positions in society, was unthinkable.

My father, who was an army doctor himself, took me in secret to the neighboring city clinic to end that pregnancy. The surgery was performed on a cold operating table with no anesthesia. It was extremely painful. We both took the bus back home without saying a word to each other. We never talked about it until very recently when he read my book.

In my book I tell at length how my forced abortion experiences were the combination of the law requiring an abortion if you are not married and the pressure of the never-told part of the culture and the society, and the value of the family, and the shame—all these gave a young woman like myself no choice.

The second time I became pregnant, it was my boyfriend's father who took me to the clinic. But by the third time I was pregnant, I was in graduate school with my soon-to-be husband. But even if you were married, you must abort unless you had a birth permit, and we couldn't get married until we had a combined age of 48. Our combined age was 44.

This time I walked in with him to a clinic in Beijing without help, nor informing any of our parents. Only after that surgery we realized that we could have actually faked our age to get a marriage certificate. We regret that we did not think of that earlier. We did get married shortly, but the baby was gone, and this was the way it worked in China.

Similarly, in my life I now see it was all threaded together, starting with Deng Xiaoping in 1978, who decided to order the one-child policy. In addition to all of these forced abortions, forced gendercide against baby girls, the policy led to the university to expel young couples who were in love and pregnant, and it led to my father and my boyfriend's father taking me to end my pregnancies, and then led to the third time I was pregnant, I knew what to do and where to go.

But it did not stop there. Now, worse yet, by the fourth time when I was pregnant, I already became the most wanted criminal of China and came to Paris in 1990. I came to the land of freedom, but I was alone and in a very bad place in my marriage. With the advice of a Chinese couple who loved very much their own child, I still did what I was taught to do: End that pregnancy, too.

So when I came to America in 1990 to testify about China's human rights abuses, Chairman Smith, you asked me during the hearing whether I knew of China's forced abortion one-child policy or not. I assumed the world knew and asked in return, "Doesn't everybody know about it?" Even at that time I did not make the connection between my own experience and whether it had anything to do with that policy. But, in fact, it is an insidious policy that causes society to immediately demand an abortion for any woman without a birth permit, married or not. To refuse would be illegal. But most unmarried women like me did not even dare to ask. I certainly did not tell anybody about it, but simply silently suffered the shame and tried to hide the secret. That is why in my country there is such a high female suicide rate, 500 women a day.

Until December 2010, when I was speaking to an American teacher about his visit to Beijing to teach the development of pregnancies, I first saw the small, but well-formed, tiny babies at 8 weeks, 10 weeks, 12 weeks. Tears started streaming down my face. It was at that moment I realized four of my little babies, not just pregnancies, were sent to the grinding tubes and turned into these pink foams; four little lives snuffed out by the government and the society that did not value life and did not think twice about all these abortions every year. In the capital city of Beijing, there are more abortions than live births to this very day, according to a report by the Chinese Academy of Social Science.

As much as I thought all along I was a freedom fighter trying to bring freedom to China and trying to save lives, I did not realize how much I was turned into the same sinful being as Chinese leaders like Deng Xiaoping and those who are enforcing the one-child policy today. And how blind I was. Even when I reached Paris, even though I was no longer under the threat of being thrown out of my school after I was already thrown out of my country, even though I was married and no longer had to hide the pregnancy in shame, I still did the only thing I knew what to do: Terminate that pregnancy. But by then I was long trained to think and act as if abortion were the way of life. There were no other choices.

To be completely truthful about the situation, you hope to bring light on what must be done to change for the future. I want to share that at that time, there was never any discussion that might have offered us another choice. There was not a movie like Juno playing in China, teaching us we could give the baby away. There were no examples like the young couple I met at Harvard Business School, who got pregnant at an American university and simply took a year off, got married, gave birth to the baby, and came back to graduate and still are having a great career. There was never anyone to inform me or pray with me on my way to the forced and coerced abortion clinics, whether in Shandong or in Beijing or in Paris, to tell us that we could save the baby's life, we could turn our spirit of despair into hope. And this is why, to this day, China is where the majority of the world's abortions are taking place every year.

Now I see how that one idea, one-child-per-family, was born to our leader, unchallenged and unstopped in a totalitarian system. Overnight it created more than 400,000 paid and brutal enforcers, helped by millions of parents of these unmarried women, volunteers—I mean, the parents are volunteers—and the tough in-laws who demand the mother to try to give birth to a baby boy at the expense of baby girls. That led to a society with the problems Dr. Hudson mentioned and this massive gender imbalance, this massive sex trafficking.

And it is not only just one person's sin, but a whole army's sin, everybody in that society, including those who try to overcome it. And that violence does not just end on the forced abortion table, it extends to the sex slave trafficked for sex slavery or child-trafficking families. It continues in every single family.

And it is a shock to me when I read the other two testimonies how each one of us all ended up with a broken marriage. And today, according to China's All Women's Federation and their survey, one-third of families suffer domestic abuse every single day. That is a glimpse of a picture of what China is becoming, its killing and violence every single day in every part and corner of the society.

So that leads to the question of what we must do now to end the killing and restore peace. It is for this reason I choose to support the bill, H.R. 2121. Once passed, the bill would give the President of the United States authority to deny entry into the U.S. for any Chinese officials enforcing forced abortions and sterilizations on unwilling women in China, an act that would be a clear crime in this country. Today these criminals would be given visas here in the United States and enjoy this great country. H.R. 2121 would also apply to family members of these officials.

This is no small matter. Just as I shared a very personal story today, this bill would become very personal to the leaders of China. One hundred thirty thousand Chinese students studied in America last year, up 30 percent compared to the year before. A majority of them came from well-to-do families, sons and daughters of officials of China. It is as if they are sensing the coming of the inevitable days of consequences and judgment. It is very likely they won't like it, and they will oppose it and possibly even threaten retaliation. But how else could we get their attention to listen?

If we do have their attention to listen, I would like them to know the truth, the truth I came to know, which is how much God loves us, for He loves the leaders of China and the people of China and the nation of China so much, He gave His one and only son, so whoever comes to know Jesus will be saved and be given eternal life, but those who refuse to know him will perish.

I am not testifying today against all the people, the leaders of China, as Chai Ling, the human rights fighter, but rather as an equal sinner with you. I can tell you with peace and in confidence that the same spiritual transformation that led me to know Jesus and to gain the freedom he has given to me through his own suffering is also available to all the people in China. I know through us we cannot make it come to an end, but we know that through the most almighty God all things are possible.

So I am concluding my testimony in peace and in hope and belief that China and its people will be set free, and will be set free soon.

Thank you.

[The prepared statement of Ms. Chai follows:]

Testimony of Chai Ling
All Girls Allowed
September 22, 2011
Subcommittee on Africa, Global Health, and Human Rights hearing:
China's One-Child Policy: The Government's Massive Crime Against Women and Unborn
Babies

Chairman Smith and Members of the Committee, thank you for giving me an opportunity to testify about this massive problem in hope and determination that one day it will come to an end.

We are here to report and mourn the loss of 400+ million lives taken in China since 1980 under the China's One-Child Policy. But I never realized until I was writing my memoir that 3 of those babies are mine.

The reason why the One Child Policy kills millions of infants and unborn children annually is because it is a "one-child **per couple**" policy. It is the "all other children must die" policy. That means most married couples are not allowed to have more than one child and of course, unmarried women in China are not allowed to have babies at all. There are 16 million forced and coerced abortions a year in China but when counting the number of abortion pills sold, possibly closer to 23 million). According to the Chinese government's own statement, 70% of these women are from unmarried. That means more than 10 million young women suffer this fate every year, up to 27 thousand every day, 19 every minute. And that is the poster of that young lady hiding her face in the IV.

The tragic equation for millions of unmarried women, especially those too young to wed is: "No marriage certificate, no birth permit. No birth permit, no baby."

The first time I became pregnant, I was 18 years old, a sophomore at Peking University. I was terrified and deeply ashamed. All I could think was a scene I saw a young couple when I first arrived Peking University, was being expelled in front of us freshman for she was found out in love and pregnant. The thought of being kicked out of school, which represented life, future, jobs, and a position in society, was unthinkable.

My father, who was an army doctor himself, took me in secret to the neighboring city's clinic to end the pregnancy. The surgery was performed on a cold operating table, with no anesthesia. It was extremely painful. We both took the bus back home without saying a word to each other. We never talked about this abortion or my second coerced abortion again for over two decades until a few days ago when he read this story in my book. In my book I tell at length how my forced abortion experience was a combination of the law requiring an abortion if you are not married and the pressure of the society, giving young women no choice.

The third time I was pregnant I was in graduate school, with my-soon-to-be-husband. But even if you are married you must abort unless you have a birth permit, and you cannot get married until you have a combined age of 48. This time I walked in with him to a clinic in Beijing, without help nor informing any of our parents. Only after that, we realized we could have tried to fake our age to and get a marriage certificate. We regret why we did not think of that earlier. We did get married shortly after. But the baby was gone. That is the way it works in China.

Similarly in my life, I now see how it was all threaded together. Started by Deng Xiaoping who decided to order the One-Child Policy, in addition to all these forced abortions, the policy led to the universities to expel young couples who were in love and pregnant, that led to my father and my boyfriend's father taking me to end my pregnancies. And that led to the third time when I was pregnant, I knew where to go and what to do. It did not stop here, worst yet, by the fourth time, when I was pregnant, I was already escaped to Paris in 1990, the land of freedom. Alone and in a very bad place in my marriage, with advice from a Chinese couple who loved very much their own child, I did what I was taught to do: ended that pregnancy too.

When I came to America in 1990 to testify about China's human rights abuses, Chairman Smith you asked me then whether I knew China's forced abortion One Child Policy. I assumed the world knew and asked in return, "Doesn't everybody know about it?" Even at that time, I did not make the connection of my experience having anything to do with that policy. It is an insidious policy causing the society to immediately demand an abortion for any woman without a birth permit, married or not. To refuse would be illegal but most unmarried women like me don't even dare to ask and certainly don't tell others about it but silently suffer in a country with the highest female suicide rate in the world, 500 woman a day every day.

Until December 2010, when I was speaking to an American teacher about his visit to China to teach about the development of pregnancies, I first saw the small but well-formed tiny babies at 8 weeks, 10 weeks, 12 weeks. Tears started stream down my face. It was at that moment, I realized four of my little babies were sent to the grinding tubes, and all turned into pink foam. Four little lives snuffed out by a Government and a society that does not value life and does not think twice with more abortions per year. In the capital city of Beijing there are more abortions than live births to this very day according to reports by the Chinese Academy of Social Sciences (CASS).

As much as I thought I was a freedom fighter trying to bring freedom and save lives, I did not realize how much I was turned into the same sinful being as Chinese's leaders like Deng Xiaoping and others who are enforcing the One-Child Policy today. And how deceptive and blinded I was: even when I reached Paris, even though I was no longer under the threat of being thrown out of my school after I was already thrown out the country, even though I was married and no longer had to hide the pregnancy in shame, still I did not appreciate the potential for that life that was within me, still I carried the mindset of China that abortion was the right choice if the circumstances made keeping the baby difficult.

For by then I was long-trained to think and act as if abortion is the way of life. To be completely truthful about the situation, in hope to shed light on what needs to change now and in the future: there was never any discussion that there might be another choice. There was not a movie like Juno playing in China teaching us that we could give the baby away. There was not one example like the one couple I met at my Harvard Business School section, that when they were pregnant at college, they could take a year off, get married and come back to graduate and still have a great career. There was never this kind of freedom nor information about the full truth of abortion to teach us that we could have a choice to give these babies life. And that is why to this day China is where the majority of the world's abortions take place every year.

It is in this reason I chose to support the bill HR 2121. Once passed, this bill would give the President of the United States freedom to deny entry to the US for any Chinese official involved in forcing abortions and sterilization on unwilling women in China, an act that would be a clear crime in this Country. But today these would-be criminals in the United States are given visas to come here and enjoy this great country. HR2121 would also apply to family members of these officials. With over 400,000 people employed by the family planning committee of China, this is no small matter. Just as I shared a very personal story today, this bill would be very personal to leaders in China. 130,000 Chinese students studied in America last year, up 30 percent from the year before. HR 2121 would change all of that. It is likely they will oppose it and possibly even threaten retaliation. But ask any member of Congress, if you were looking in the face of the person who just injected a needle of deadly poison into the brain of a near full term 8 month old baby in the womb of its mother as shown on Al Jazerra television would you grant them a Visa to come from China to the United States? If not, then why is there no law to make sure it does not happen?

I am not here to testify against you, the leaders of China, as Chai Ling, the human rights fighter; but as an equal sinner with you. I can tell you with peace and confidence that a spiritual transformation awaits you if you put your faith in Christ Jesus you will have the courage to change and demand change of others, and you will see clearly that you don't need to act like Deng Xiaoping in 1989, feeling that he had no other choice. You can still turn and end this policy, and can start reshaping the culture of China to value all women, their choice, and children's lives.

Freedom is awaiting you as it is awaiting 1.3 billion other Chinese men and women under your watch. Though evil blinded me and blinded all of us to do evil, God wants us to see, to be set free, and to experience his love and receive eternal life.

Isaiah 61

The Spirit of the Lord GOD is upon me,
  because the LORD has anointed me
to bring good news to the poor;[a]
  he has sent me to bind up the brokenhearted,
to proclaim liberty to the captives,
  and the opening of the prison to those who are bound;[b]
2 to proclaim the year of the LORD's favor,
  and the day of vengeance of our God;
  to comfort all who mourn;
3 to grant to those who mourn in Zion—
  to give them a beautiful headdress instead of ashes,
the oil of gladness instead of mourning,
  the garment of praise instead of a faint spirit;
that they may be called oaks of righteousness,
  the planting of the LORD, that he may be glorified.[c]
4 They shall build up the ancient ruins;
  they shall raise up the former devastations;
they shall repair the ruined cities,
  the devastations of many generations.

———————

Mr. SMITH. Thank you very much, Ms. Chai. To love and to wish well and reconciliation on those who have so abused you and the women of China is truly miraculous. So thank you for that witness.

Ms. CHAI. You are very welcome.

Mr. SMITH. Ms. Littlejohn.

STATEMENT OF MS. REGGIE LITTLEJOHN, FOUNDER AND PRESIDENT, WOMEN'S RIGHTS WITHOUT FRONTIERS

Ms. LITTLEJOHN. Mr. Chairman, Representative Fortenberry, honorable members of the subcommittee, I am grateful for this opportunity to testify and for the fact that we can even talk about these things in the United States. Basically every single thing that has been said so far in this hearing would be considered to be a state secret in China, and all of us would be detained. And so I am grateful to this committee and this Nation that we can speak out. And, in fact, people like Chen Guangcheng, when they try to speak out, end up in the deplorable conditions which I will describe later on, but because we have the ability to speak out, I feel that we have the moral obligation to speak out.

I have been asked to brief the subcommittee on the findings of our new report, to testify regarding the impact of coercive enforcement of China's one-child policy on human rights, and to comment on the case of Chen Guangcheng.

So, this is our new report on the one-child policy. It is released today. It is called "China's One-Child Policy: New Evidence of Coercion—Forced Abortion, Sterilization, Contraception, and the Practice of Implication," which is something I learned about in researching this report.

Mr. SMITH. Without objection, your report will be made part of the record.

Ms. LITTLEJOHN. I hope it will be. I heard is it is a little long to be made. But I thank you, Mr. Chairman.

In this report are 13 new documented cases that are just as grievous as the cases that we have heard today. In this report we have cases of forced abortion, one woman at 8 months, another woman forcibly aborted with twins at 8½ months; forced sterilization; forced contraception. And these forced contraceptions are not simply the installation of IUDs, which can be very painful, and even, as the witnesses have said today, these IUDs can be installed even though there are medical complications that contraindicate such an installation. But people—the lack of an IUD is used as an excuse for family planning cadres to come in and maim people. I have got a case in here where somebody's mother-in-law literally had her hand almost broken in half because her daughter-in-law supposedly didn't have an IUD.

We have got pictures of family planning police. It looks like a military regiment; family planning jail cells; the demolition of homes, even by relatives. There is a woman here who missed a pregnancy check, and her own relatives were forced to demolish her home. We have pictures of that.

This report also contains accounts of a couple who were brutally tortured because the woman missed a pregnancy check by one day. She was one day late. A man whose head was smashed open and who is now permanently disabled because his wife had a second child. I will show this briefly. But this report is filled with photographs like this. And a father who was beaten to death because his son was suspected of having a second child.

Now, we went back and forth on this, and finally we did choose to release the names of the perpetrators of these crimes. So this report has at least several dozen names of the actual human beings who perpetrated these crimes, what they did, what their position was at that time. They are identifiable. And I did this in consultation with China Aid. I want to thank China Aid for their substantial contribution to this report. But basically these people need to be held accountable.

Again, Representative Smith, you have sponsored the China Democracy Promotion Act of 2011, which, if passed, people such as these people who have gone around doing heinous crimes against humanity will not be allowed free access to American soil.

Human rights violations. In addition to forced abortion, gendercide and female suicide, China's one-child policy gives rise to several other serious human rights violations. Number one, human trafficking and sexual slavery. Because of the abortion, abandonment and infanticide of baby girls, there are an estimated 37 million more Chinese men than there are women. This gender imbalance caused by gendercide is perhaps the driving force behind human trafficking and sexual slavery in China. And according to the 2011 TIP Report, the Trafficking in Persons Report, women and children from neighboring countries, including Burma, Vietnam, Laos, Mongolia, Russia and North Korea, and from locations as far as Romania and Zimbabwe, are reportedly trafficked into China for commercial sexual exploitation and forced labor.

Women's Rights Without Frontiers has a petition against forced abortion and sexual slavery in China, and we have printed out the signatories here. We have more than 9,000 from 80 countries. So this is a genuinely international outcry.

Infanticide. Last year, crematorium workers in Guangdong Province found an infant crying in a medical waste receptacle on the way to the crematorium. When they opened it, they found a little baby boy who had cotton stuffed down his throat. Horrified, they sent that baby boy back to the hospital, perfectly healthy, and then that boy was returned to them later that day without any explanation of the cause of death.

In a separate incident, Xinhua reported that 21 bodies of fetuses and babies were found discarded in a river in east China last year. Xinhua News stated, "The bodies may have been dumped by cleaners from local hospitals after abortions and induced labor. Such dead bodies are treated as medical waste by hospitals."

Forced sterilization. The first case in my new report is of a woman who was literally running away from a forced sterilization and was grabbed and dragged back to the hospital. These forced sterilizations are not done by highly trained gynecological surgeons. They are done under horrible conditions. Women frequently get massive infections, and it ruins their health for the rest their lives.

So I asked organizations like UNFPA and International Planned Parenthood, if they truly stand for choice, if they truly stand for women's reproductive rights and women's reproductive health, how come they aren't jumping up and down about forced sterilization in China?

For example, there was a 20-day campaign launched April 7th of 2010 in Puning City, Guandong Province, aimed to sterilize 9,559 people, and they detained 1,300 people in that forced sterilization campaign. That campaign was publicized in the London Times. Everybody knew about it. Where was UNFPA? Where was IPPF when this was going on, if they truly are promoting voluntarism in China?

Implication. Now, that is something new that I learned in researching this report. The practice of implication means if one person is a violator of the one-child policy, then their entire extended family is implicated or punished. So, for example, if I were illegally pregnant, my husband, my parents, his parents, our grandparents, our aunts, uncles, nieces, nephews, the entire extended family can have their homes destroyed. In this one incident, case 12 in Fujian Province, family planning officials beat a father to death on the suspicion that his son might have a second child. That is implication.

Then in another case, the extended family were all dragged in to something called the Family Planning Learning Center, and they were tortured for days on end, and then they were charged tuition, which also brings up the issue of corruption, which I think is a major driving force behind keeping the one-child policy in place. People are making a lot of money off of this.

Another thing that has come to the forefront to me, we all know that China's one-child policy causes more violence toward women and girls than any other official policy on Earth or any other official policy in the world. But you know what? China's one-child policy also causes tremendous violence against men, and that comes out in this report. It is through the implication that this occurs.

Recently, just this year in Linyi County, there was a man who was murdered by family planning police. They had come to seize his sister for a forced abortion. She wasn't home, so they started beating his father. So when he tried to defend his father, one of the family planning officials just took a knife and stabbed him in the chest, and he died. And these things happen with impunity. People are not prosecuted. They are not held accountable. I would say that really the spirit of the Red Guard lives on in the family planning police.

Chen Guangcheng. Blind activist Chen Guangcheng was arrested in 2006 for exposing the fact that there were 130,000 forced abortions and forced sterilizations in just one county, Linyi County, and Ji Yeqing, who just testified, was just 1 of those 130,000. So the suffering that was caused by this is just incalculable. He was named by Time Magazine as one of 2006's top 100 people who shape our world, and was also nominated for the Nobel Peace Prize.

As you know, for his activism against forced abortion in China, he then was imprisoned 4 years, 3 months, jailed, tortured, denied medical treatment, and also got an intestinal condition in the jail. And when he was released in September 2010, he and his wife were again beaten and tortured and denied medical treatment when they got a video out about the conditions of their house arrest.

Now, the latest on him is, as you know, they turned basically not only his home, but the entire village into a prison. So around his home there are 22 cadres every 8 hours, 66 cadres every 24 hours, just watching him, making sure nobody goes in, nobody comes out. He is completely sealed off from the world. But according to several Radio Free Asia reports, number one, they built like a separate prison for him that they are going to move him to; number two, his 6-year-old daughter has been denied an education; and, number three, his brother has been detained as well, and there is a group of activists who tried to visit him just this past week who were beaten and detained.

So Bob Fu of the China Aid Association and Women's Rights Without Frontiers are spearheading an effort to free Chen Guangcheng. We already have over 5,000 signatures from a couple dozen countries to free him. And he is being starved; he is sick; he is beaten, tortured, denied medical treatment. His wife was able to get a letter out a couple months ago about his condition, saying that she was worried he wasn't going to survive. We haven't heard anything from them since then, other than the fact they are going to be put into their own personal prison. But it is absolutely urgent that Chen Guangcheng be freed.

Now, I just want to make one comment about China possibly moving to a two-child policy. I have heard people—nobody here, but people say, well, wouldn't it be okay if they had a two-child policy? My answer is no, for several reasons.

Number one, already much of the country can have a second child. In the countryside, if your first child is a girl, you can try for a boy on your second child. And what that has done is it has given rise to gendercide. The worst gender imbalances happen when the couple has a girl as the first child, and then they try for a boy on the second child. There are many areas of China where that ratio is 160 boys born to 100 girls born. So I don't think that saying, oh, everything will be solved if they have a second child.

Secondly, for me, the cornerstone of the one-child policy is not how many children are allowed, is it one child, is it two children. It is, number one, the fact that the government is imposing its will on something that should be a family decision; and, number two, the coercion with which it is enforced.

In China, a woman's body is not her own. It is in the domain of the state. And until the Chinese family planning officials stop functioning as womb police, the nation of China will not be free.

Thank you.

[The prepared statement of Ms. Littlejohn follows:]

Post Office Box 54401, San Jose, CA 95154, 310.592.5722
www.womensrightswithoutfrontiers.org

The Coercive Enforcement of China's One Child Policy – Systematic, Institutionalized Violence Against Women and Families

Testimony of Reggie Littlejohn, President
Women's Rights Without Frontiers
September 22, 2011
House Committee on Foreign Affairs,
Subcommittee on Africa, Global Health, and Human Rights

Honorable members of the Sub-Committee, ladies and gentlemen, I am grateful for this opportunity to testify here today. During a sensitive time in engaging the People's Republic of China (PRC) on human rights issues, I am truly moved by continuing concern of those present for the suffering of the people of China.

I have been asked to brief the Sub-Committee on the findings of our new report, to testify regarding the impact of the coercive enforcement of China's One Child Policy on human rights, and to comment on the case of Chen Guangcheng.

New Report on the One Child Policy

Women's Rights Without Frontiers released our new report today -- "China's One Child Policy: New Evidence of Coercion – Forced Abortion, Sterilization, Contraception, and the practice of Implication." In this report are thirteen new, documented cases of coercion: forced abortion (including one woman at eight months and another carrying twins at 8 ½ months), forced sterilization, forced contraception, the use of abortion and sterilization quotas, Family Planning Police, Family Planning jail cells, the demolition of homes (even by relatives, for missing a pregnancy check), the use of "implication" (detention, torture and fining of relatives of "violators"). The report contains accounts of a couple brutally tortured for missing a pregnancy check by one day; a man whose head was smashed open and who is now permanently disabled because his wife had a second child; a father who was beaten to death because his son was suspected of having a second child.

We have chosen to release the names of the perpetrators of these Crimes Against Humanity, so that they can be held accountable before the world. This report contains dozens of their names, as well as details of their crimes.

The "China Democracy Promotion Act of 2011," if passed, would enable the President to deny entry into the U.S. for Chinese nationals, such as these, who have "committed human rights abuses" against people in China, including anyone who "has participated in the imposition of . . . China's coercive birth limitation policy."

Human Rights Violations
In addition to forced abortion, gendercide, and female suicide, China's One Child Policy gives rise to several other serious human rights violations:

Human Trafficking and Sexual Slavery. Because of abortion, abandonment, and infanticide of baby girls, there are an estimated 37 million Chinese men who will never marry because they cannot find wives. This gender imbalance is a powerful, driving force behind trafficking in women and sexual slavery from nations surrounding China. According to the 2011 Trafficking in Person (TIP) Report, China is on the Tier 2 Watch List: a source, destination and transit country for trafficked people. "Women and children from neighboring countries including Burma, Vietnam, Laos, Mongolia, Russia, and North Korea, and from locations as far as Romania and Zimbabwe are reportedly trafficked to China for commercial sexual exploitation and forced labor."[i]

Women's Rights Without Frontiers has a petition against forced abortion and sexual slavery in China. We now have more than 9,000 signatures from 80 nations around the world – a truly international outcry.[ii]

Infanticide. Last year, crematorium workers in Guangdong Province found an infant crying in a "medical waste" receptacle on its way to being cremated, reports Xinhua, China's official news agency. The crematorium workers immediately sent the infant back to the hospital. Later that day, the hospital sent the infant back to the crematorium, dead. The hospital offered no explanation of the cause of death.[iii]

Xinhua reported that 21 bodies of fetuses and babies were found discarded in a river in East China. Xinhua News stated, "the bodies may have been dumped by cleaners from local hospitals after abortions and induced labor. Such dead bodies are treated as 'medical waste' by hospitals."[iv]

Forced Sterilization. As in Case One of our new report, women are literally dragged off the street, strapped down to tables and forcibly sterilized. According to the London Times, Family Planning Authorities have detained 1300 people in a campaign to sterilize nearly 10,000 people in Puning City, Guandong Province.[v]

The twenty-day campaign, launched April 7, is well along in achieving its goal of 9,559 sterilizations. "A doctor in Daba village said that his team was working flat out, beginning sterilizations every day at 8 am and working straight through until 4 am the following day." What's the hurry? Officials in Puning may fail in their bid for promotion to a second tier county "if they cannot meet all quotas," according to The London Times.

"Implication." Case Six of WRWF's new report describes the practice of "Implication," which means that if anyone breaks the family planning policy, their entire extended family is held responsible. Parents, grandparents, siblings, aunts and uncles, cousins, nieces and nephews can be detained, fined and tortured. In an area of Fujian Province in 2008, the extended family of a Family Planning "violator" were seized and forced to attend a "Family Planning Learning Class," where they were tortured and then charged "tuition."

Violence Against Men. The practice of implication causes violence not only against women, but also against men. Case Seven of our report gives the account of a couple with a second child in Henan Province. Family planning police smashed the father in the head with a bottle. He is now permanently disabled. In Case Twelve, in Jiangsu Province, Family Planning Officials beat a farmer to death because his son was suspected of having an extra child. Recently, in Linyi County, Shandong Province, near where Chen Guangcheng lives, a Family Planning Official murdered a man. They had come to seize his sister for a forced sterilization. Failing to find her, they started to beat their father. When the man defended his father, one of the Officials plunged a knife in his heart, and he died.[vi]

Most often, Family Planning Officials are not prosecuted for their crimes, but act with impunity. The spirit of the Red Guard lives on in the Family Planning Police.

Despite overwhelming evidence to the contrary,[vii] in January of this year, President Hu Jintao denied to Rep. Ileana Ros-Lehtinen that China has a forced abortion policy.[viii] Moreover, China has stated that it will continue its One Child Policy for "decades" to come.[ix]

Chen Guangcheng

Blind activist Chen Guangcheng was arrested in 2006 for helping to expose the Chinese government's use of forced sterilization and abortions to enforce its "One Child Policy." He amassed evidence that 130,000 forced abortions and involuntary sterilizations were performed on women in Linyi County, Shandong Province in a single year. *Time Magazine* named him one of "2006's Top 100 People Who Shape Our World" and he was given the 2007 Magsaysay award, known as Asia's Nobel Prize.

Chen spent four years, three months in prison. His defense lawyers were detained on the eve of trial. After his September 2010 release, he continues to serve a sentence of home detention. Both in prison and under house arrest, Chen experienced mistreatment and beatings. He suffers from a chronic, debilitating intestinal illness for which he has been denied treatment.

According to a February, 2011 video testimony provided by Chen smuggled out of China, 66 security police surround his home constantly. He and his wife are not allowed sufficient food and are isolated from all outside contact. No one can enter or leave their home, except officials, who can enter at any time, without notice.

After the video's release, Chen and his wife were severely beaten,[x] and lawyers who organized to help him were detained, beaten, and disappeared, including prominent lawyers Jiang Tianyong and Teng Biao. Foreign journalists who tried to visit Chen have been physically barred from entering his village. A CNN report showed unidentified security officers pushing a journalist and throwing rocks at him to prevent him from entering Chen's village.

The letter written by Chen's wife on June 15, 2011 indicates the need for urgent and immediate action to help Chen Guancheng and his wife Yuan Wejing.

We have received evidence that blind activist Chen Guangcheng's health is in serious jeopardy because of repeated beatings and the malnutrition he suffers in house detention. According to a letter written by Chen's wife, and smuggled out of China, Chen faces constant physical and psychological abuse, does not get sufficient food or nourishment, and is denied proper medical treatment. Foreign journalists have been forcibly denied access to him and lawyers who tried to help Chen were beaten and detained in February 2011.[xi]

Chen and his family will be transferred to a small prison built specifically for them, according to a Radio Free Asia report.[xii]

Activist He Peirong stated that the couple will be forcibly removed from their home and transferred to a building "which basically amounts to a jail" so that authorities can "keep tighter controls on them." Their young son, living with relatives, was reportedly strip-searched leaving the family home.

Just in the past week, a couple of human rights campaigners seeking to see Chen were beaten and detained.[xiii] Earlier this month, police detained Chen's brother, who was meeting with activists.[xiv] Chen's six year old daughter was denied the right to an education.[xv]

Women's Rights Without Frontiers and the China Aid Association are spearheading an international effort to free Chen Guangcheng. Thus far, we have collected 5161 signatures from 28 countries.[xvi]

WRWF congratulates Rep. Chris Smith on his successful sponsorship last July of an amendment to the State Department Appropriation Bill, in support of Chen Guangcheng and his family. This amendment, which passed unanimously, urges the Chinese government to stop harassing the Chen family, to release them from house arrest, and to arrange for immediate medical treatment. It further urges the Obama administration to arrange diplomatic visits to the Chen family. Beyond this, it highlights the tragedy of forced abortion and coercive family planning in China. This amendment comes just in time, as Chen's health is frail and deteriorating rapidly. [xvii]

Conclusion

In China, a woman's body is not her own. It belongs to the state. A woman's womb is the most intimate part of her body – physically, emotionally and spiritually. For the Chinese Communist Party to act as "womb police" and crush the life inside her is a heinous crime against humanity.

[i] Trafficking in Persons Report, Released 6/27/11
http://www.state.gov/g/tip/rls/tiprpt/2011/164231.htm

[ii] To view WRWF's online petition to end forced abortion an sexual slavery in China, click here:
http://www.womensrightswithoutfrontiers.org/index.php?nav=sign_our_petition

[iii] "Aborted Baby Cries Before Cremation," Australian Women Online, 6/3/10
http://www.australianwomenonline.com/forced-abortion-and-sterlisation-in-china/

[iv] Two Detained as Baby Bodies Wash Ashore in China River.
http://www.nypost.com/p/news/international/baby_bodies_wash_ashore_in_china_qA5DSSYsQTYQ2JQcA7Ad3M

[v] China's Forced Sterilization Campaign is a Crime Against Humanity. 5/4/10
http://www.theepochtimes.com/n2/content/view/34698/

[vi] "Family Planning Official Stabs Man to Death." 4/5/11
http://www.womensrightswithoutfrontiers.org/blog/?p=147

[vii] Appalling Youtube Video, China: Forced Abortion at Eight Months, 10/20/10,
http://www.youtube.com/watch?v=xIycnQ-njlQ

[viii] Hu Denies Forced Abortions: US Lawmaker (AFPP), 1/20/11
http://www.google.com/hostednews/afp/article/ALeqM5j3Mh3tnXMcd0WNe-hRScjwTSjTdg?docId=CNG.0dd9bfe0c5ee86343c03c93188764bfa.b61

[ix] State Media: China to Stick with One Child Policy, USA Today, 9/27/10
http://www.usatoday.com/news/world/2010-09-27-china-one-child-policy_N.htm

[x] Letter Alleges Beating of Chinese Activist and Wife, 6/18/11
http://www.nytimes.com/2011/06/18/world/asia/18china.html

[xi] A copy of the original letter in Mandarin can be obtained by emailing ChinaAid at bobfu@chinaaid.org
or by calling 267.205.5210. An English translation can be found here:
http://www.womensrightswithoutfrontiers.org/index.php?nav=yuan-weijing
Here is a three minute video calling for urgent action:
Free Chen Guangcheng! http://www.youtube.com/watch?v=OpVJidDqVJo

[xii] See, 'Jail' Built for Activist, Family, 8/30/11
http://www.rfa.org/english/news/china/jail-08302011123544.html

[xiii] "Chen Supporters Attacked." 9/19/11
http://www.rfa.org/english/news/china/attacked-09192011123000.html

[xiv] "Police Detain Nanjing Activists," 9/8/11
http://www.rfa.org/english/news/china/activists-09082011152203.html?searchterm=None

[xv] "Daughter of Blind Chinese Human Rights Lawyer Deprived of Schooling," 9/8/11
http://www.theepochtimes.com/n2/china-news/daughter-of-blind-chinese-human-rights-lawyer-deprived-of-schooling-61278.html

[xvi] The petition to free Chen Guangcheng can be found here:
http://www.womensrightswithoutfrontiers.org/index.php?nav=sign_our_petition

[xvii] "Amendment for Blind Activist Chen Guangcheng Passes Today," 7/22/11
http://www.womensrightswithoutfrontiers.org/blog/?p=316

Mr. SMITH. Ms. Littlejohn, thank you so much. Thank you for your report, and for the accuracy and the detail and the earnestness that you bring to this, and for your legal representation of those women who have been so cruelly mistreated by the Chinese Government.

I have so many questions, but let me just begin with a few. When the U.S. Department of State under John Negroponte, who was then the point person for the Bush administration, made its finding, there were a number of very important aspects to that finding with regards to international complicity in these crimes against women and children. And one of those was that programming by NGOs and by regional groups out of the UNFPA in China is always in the context of Chinese law. They follow Chinese law.

When we hear about the so-called choice offered to women in those areas, those counties where the UNFPA has a presence, the only choice is what method may be adopted, what type of contraceptive, IUD or some other means. But with resoluteness, to use the word of the Chinese system, women are still held to one child, they are coerced to abort, and they are coerced to have—whether it be an IUD or some other means.

I am amazed to this day how even the Washington Post, when it did a big story about how the UNFPA and China itself is offering more choice, failed to see that the coercive elements are as harsh and as brutal as ever, just choose your poison. There is no choice for the individual woman.

They also point out, and I think this is important, the 2000 law—this is the finding that was done pursuant to the Kemp-Kasten language—is not just about harsh controlling of the size of the population, but to improve its quality. And when that law went into effect, I asked the Holocaust Museum their view and analysis of this eugenics policy, and they said it comported with what the Nazis did, trying to make a better Chinese man and woman by weeding out the undesirables. Unfortunately, the UNFPA and others are completely complicit in ensuring that those who might have some disability do not see the light of day and are not born.

Any comments you might have on that, I would appreciate that.

The two women, Ms. Ji and Ms. Liu, who spoke, the idea that the factory—and anyone who would like to comment on this—actually as far as back as Michael Weiskopf's incisive three-part series in the mid-1980s in the Washington Post, the former bureau chief for the Washington Post, he wrote those articles as he was leaving, talked about how this is implemented at the factory level; that women are subjected to very degrading inspections, their menstrual cycles are monitored, and if they are found to be pregnant without a birth allowed certificate, they are then forcibly aborted.

If you could speak to factories and whether or not U.S. companies, which have a huge factory presence in China, might be involved in this as well. Are they part of the factory clinic or on the factory floor?

Ms. Liu talked about how she was reported by her coworkers to be pregnant. We have U.S. factories there. Are reportings going on about illegal children, and are they forcibly aborted?

Dr. Hudson, you talked about the coming economic hardship in China. Dr. Eberstadt did testify recently at a hearing I chaired, and he talked about this huge disproportionality of not just missing girls and women, as you call it the missing daughters, but also about this heavily skewed senior population. I have never seen this on CNBC; I have never seen any analysis by the Fed or anyone else about this sinkhole of economic progress coming to a grinding halt in China. And yet, as I think you have indicated, it is right around the corner.

Dr. Hudson, could you answer the question, has our Pentagon— has there been any interest shown anywhere, the Army War College, about the grave implications for potential war? As you said in your testimony, and you said it so eloquently, if I can just find it, on the last page, and that is, might a situation develop where the government sees a way to kill two birds with one stone, seizing a greater share of international power through successful international use of force, while also thinning the ranks of the bare branches through attrition or warfare?

That is a profound statement. Who is listening to that at the Pentagon, at the United Nations, for example, or anywhere else? I am going to ask the Armed Services Committee to hold a hearing on these implications. This is something that is present today, but only gets exacerbated as the days move forward.

So, Dr. Hudson, maybe you could speak to that. I have many other questions, but as some opening questions.

Before you do, I would like to also just get on the record, I do believe that population control has turned out to be a weapon of mass destruction. More children, more women, more persons have died as a direct result of that, and it could happen here.

Ted Turner recently said that we need in America, the United States, to adopt a one-child-per-couple policy. A man from Planned Parenthood wrote—and I have a copy of what he said, where he said, let me just get it—a couple of weeks ago, Executive Vice President Norman Fleishman: "China's 'one child' policy . . . is a start . . . the world is doomed to strangle among the coils of pitiless exponential growth." Ted Turner has said it and said it repeatedly. And on the IPPF Web site, the International Planned Parenthood Web site, the Kenyan Planning Permanent Secretary Edward Sambili said, "We might be forced to halt the free primary education programme because some parents are exploiting it by getting many children . . .". Then he even says maybe we ought to look at food as well as something that might be deprived. All coming out of China.

So, Dr. Hudson.

Ms. HUDSON. Wow, I find that very interesting. There are some cultural winds blowing through the West that do bear some uncanny echoes with this notion that the government has a role in limiting birth, and so I am not going to dismiss that in the least.

For example, I remember once at an academic conference asking whether it would be possible for the United States to outlaw sex-selective abortion. There is a bit of a problem, yes, but there isn't a huge problem at this point, so why not harvest the low-hanging fruit and go on the record as a nation that bans sex-selective abortion? I was laughed at as being politically naive; that it would be impossible in the United States or any advanced country to place any infringements whatsoever on a woman's right to choose.

But it is not just an issue of choice. Whenever we talk about women's choices, we have to look at the context in which those choices are taking place. And I think the one-child policy is a perfect example of how we have heard that a woman's choice was not actually a choice at all. So I worry that we can't even have this conversation in the United States of America; that it is somehow politically incorrect to raise these issues, even though I believe these are terribly important issues.

You asked, did the Pentagon? No, not really. There was a few years ago DTRA, the Defense Threat Reduction Agency, did ask for sort of a think paper from me and my colleague, and that pretty much has been it. So I would be happy to be involved in any future endeavors that you might have to bring this to the attention of those whose job it is to think about security trends in the world.

I know it seems somehow anachronistic to somehow suggest that demographic forces may play a role in future security scenarios. I myself don't see it as anachronistic. I see it as realistic to think about demographic trends and their intersection with security and with economic trends as well. So please keep me apprised of any opportunities to bring these issues to the attention of those who need to know. I would be grateful for that.

Mr. SMITH. On that issue I will ask for a classified briefing to find out what, if anything, is being done, and will also ask Buck McKeon, who is the chairman of the Armed Services Committee, if his committee could look into this as well and start asking some questions.

Ms. HUDSON. I want to just apologize in advance if I have to run.

Mr. SMITH. I know you have a plane to catch. Thank you.

Ms. LITTLEJOHN. I just wanted to follow up on Dr. Hudson's remark about sex-selective abortion and the conversation that she had with those who say that is part of a woman's right to choose.

Because of sex-selective abortion, or gendercide, there is one U.N. expert who actually estimated there are 200 million women missing, and most of those women are missing from Asia, that have this extremely oppressive son preference. And these women are not choosing to abort their daughters. They are being—I would argue that sex-selective abortion in Asia, which is where most of it happens, is a species of forced abortion. These women do not have a choice. If they already have a girl, or even if they don't already have a girl, they are under tremendous pressure from sometimes their husbands, their in-laws, their own parents, whatever. So for people to abandon those women for the rare woman who will choose to have a sex-selective abortion, say this is a woman's choice, and meanwhile abandoning the 99 percent that are being forced to do this, I think, is not a helpful approach to the issue.

Mr. SMITH. Ms. Chai?

Ms. CHAI. Yes. Actually I was—maybe I am naive. I saw in June when five U.N. organizations who tend to be prochoice organizations, you know, the World Health Organization, UNFPA, U.N. Women, Human Rights, I think there is one more, they all jointly come together to make a declaration against gendercide, including gender-based selective abortions. I felt that was a great encouragement and gives hope that maybe the U.N. organizations are starting to wake up to this massive problem the world has created.

Mr. SMITH. With respect, though, I read that report very carefully, and it was written in a way that, in my opinion, paid lip service to genocide. But if the child in utero is completely expendable, as Dr. Hudson said, it is so politically incorrect to suggest that killing an unborn baby because she happens to be a girl.

There is a bill which has been introduced by Trent Franks of, which I and my colleagues here are cosponsors of, that would outlaw it. And Obama would veto it—no doubt about it, if we get it passed. The Senate probably wouldn't even take it up. But in reading that report—and I take great fault with the U.N. agencies, including the UNFPA that signed it, they offer several times that this, in no way, should encumber the unfettered right to choose an abortion for whatever reason.

Hillary Clinton, and I hope the next time she testifies, I will certainly ask her this, she has changed her rhetoric, not that it was ever clear or precise—when it comes to condemning what goes on in China. But she made it very clear that she is against gendercide when it deals with infanticide; in other words, the born young girl. So don't kill the baby at birth; don't smother her, which we all absolutely agree with, but not before birth. She will not take a stand. And I hope she hears this and changes her opinion about the girl who was selected for extermination who is in utero, simply because she is a girl. Very, very disturbing.

Even Senator Feinstein, when she made statements during a gubernatorial race years ago, made a comment which, at first encouraged all of us that sex selection abortion was cruelty and wrong, and the pro-abortion NGOs and her opponent, who was trying to be more pro-abortion than thou, got on her case and she backtracked and became very, very quiet, if you will, and worse, no longer supporting the outlawing of sex selection abortions. It is an American problem too. The diaspora are coming in from some countries, are increasingly using sex selection abortions as a means to choose the gender of their newborn, by killing the others. So it is a very, very disturbing trend. I have other questions. But as a courtesy to my colleagues—we are joined by Ann Marie Buerkle, who is both a nurse and a lawyer, so she brings both of those professions in terms of her experience. But I would like to yield to my good friend and colleague, the vice chair of the subcommittee, Mr. Fortenberry.

Mr. FORTENBERRY. Thank you, Mr. Chairman. Again, let me reiterate my sincere thanks for your willingness to testify today. Those of us who have been on the subcommittee that looks at global human rights issues frankly are barraged constantly with such an array of assaults on human dignity, it can almost dull the conscience. But I have to share with you that today's hearing has, you know, in such a laser-like fashion, affected me and informed me and hurt me as to the difficulties and pain that you all have gone through and that millions of people who are under this repression are continuing to suffer that it stands out as one of the most grotesque abuses against humanity today.

Perhaps it is because we are talking about something that is conceived in love and should bring about joy. But then is this force to be ripped out by an authoritarian cause greater than that individual life, greater than that love between the couple and perhaps that is why it is so deeply disturbing.

So again, let me say thank you for your courage and your leadership in this regard. Mr. Chairman, I think it should be pointed out that, here we are in America. But Ms. Liu is still behind a closed area here because she fears reprisals potentially taken against those she loves back in China. This is simply an outrage and the most grievous assault on human dignity. Thank you, Mr. Chairman, for your willingness to probe this more deeply.

How can we sit by idly and not look at this in the face and not got our minds around this horror and not act? And in that regard, I want to follow up with your question, Mr. Chairman, that I don't think was sufficiently unpacked. But I want to hear any thoughts that you may have in terms of U.S. companies who may be complicit inadvertently, I assume—perhaps not, in this forced factory model of monitoring the privacy of women's own intimate relations as well as the status of them as mothers. Can you provide more information or thoughts on that? Yes.

Ms. LITTLEJOHN. I can provide more thoughts. I cannot provide more information. I think we need more information. I think that this is a very, very fruitful avenue to pursue. I believe that the one-child policy is a crime against humanity. It falls within the definition. The legal definition of a crime against humanity, as defined by The Hague and the International Criminal Court is, it has to be a serious human rights violation; and forced sterilization and forced pregnancy are already in the list. So forced abortion, there is no legal reason to exclude it.

So it is a serious human rights violation perpetrated or tolerated by a regime against a civilian population. So even if the Chinese Communist Party says, well, we aren't doing this. It is just the people in the hinterlands. Well, they are tolerating it because, for example, in that whole thing with the Puning forced sterilization campaign that went on for 20 days, China did nothing to stop it. Okay. So let's say that this is a crime against humanity and let's say that American corporations are doing business and have factories in China that are complicit with it. Okay. I could see lawsuits against American corporations charging them criminally with crimes against humanity, number one. And number two——

Mr. FORTENBERRY. Do you think that American companies have very close proximity in terms of ownership or even entanglements with management where there are fertility hall monitors on a factory floor?

Ms. LITTLEJOHN. That is what we need to find out. See, this is something that is going to take investigation and it is probably going to take undercover investigation, you know? I think it would be great if there could be teams inside of China.

Mr. FORTENBERRY. Can you imagine this going on in America?

Ms. LITTLEJOHN. No.

Mr. FORTENBERRY. We can't even imagine that this could happen in this country. It is inconceivable. We can't get our minds around it, that you would have a company that monitors a woman's fertility and forces, as you said, undignified exposure on a factory floor. That is not work. That is not employment. That is a form of slavery.

Ms. CHAI. Yes.

Mr. FORTENBERRY. I am sorry to interrupt you but I think you are right. I mean, to continue to explore this possibility I think would highlight the larger problem in the society and put all of us on notice in America, that if we are going to do something about this, this is the place to start. We cannot directly cooperate in this.

Mr. SMITH. If you would yield briefly. In your answer, if you could give whether or not you would advise us to work on legislation that would develop a code of conduct, like the Sullivan Principles for South Africa, like the MacBride Principles for Northern Ireland, that would get to the heart of the complicity. And I know Mr. Fortenberry and I and Ms. Buerkle, I am sure, and others could rally around such a code. I asked that question one time on a trip to Beijing with the U.S. Chamber of Commerce in Beijing. And all but one person—most of them wouldn't say anything—and then one individual, one of the business reps, the U.S. reps in Beijing said, "Oh, but we made sure that that was out of what we agreed to when we came here." And the others did not say that they agreed to take out monitoring women's menstrual cycles and the like. So a code of conduct we could use.

Mr. FORTENBERRY. Yes. Thank you. That is a good idea.

Ms. LITTLEJOHN. People hear about the reality, the brutal reality behind the one-child policy, and it makes us feel outraged and it makes us feel like we want to do something. But we feel so impotent because China is a sovereign nation. We can't really do anything. Well, we can do something, okay? I love the idea of some kind of legislation that would require companies doing business in China to not be complicit with crimes against humanity, for example. And I think that we could have some kind of a corporate social responsibility requirement that, when American companies do business in a foreign nation—you know, it could be even broader than China, that they cannot be engaging in crimes against humanity, even if those crimes are in conformance with the laws of that country. I mean, there is a direct analogy to Nazi Germany. You know, should American corporations be able to go to Nazi Germany and be complicit with the holocaust even though it was the law of the land? The answer is no.

Mr. FORTENBERRY. Thank you, Mr. Chairman.

Mr. SMITH. Thank you very much. Ms. Buerkle.

Ms. CHAI. Mr. Fortenberry, I would like to comment on your brilliant question, which is absolutely right on target. It is something that I would have loved to have seen legislation taking place long ago. I couldn't find the right term. I even talked to some experts on Capitol Hill—actually, I think I spoke to one of your staff a few months ago, saying, what can we do to either modify the Anticorruption Act or something for all foreign companies who conduct business in China to require and demand the local working conditions to be in compliance to a certain level of humanity standards? And that was driven by an article I think in either The Wall Street Journal or New York Times about a factory where they have such a high suicide rate, to the point where the factory erected big barbed wires and started bringing psychological counselors to come in.

We don't exactly know what are the reasons to force the people to jump through the building to kill themselves. But we believe forced abortions, this kind of inhumane treatment, abuses toward young women through all levels might be a cause or a reason toward that. And that was a company that basically supplied the majority of all the components that go into Apple computers, goes into iPads, goes into iPhones. And none of those workers could ever afford a product like that that they were producing or making. The suggestion was, if we have a law, none of the U.S. companies can go do these kinds of things for a country, that would provide the level playing field. And otherwise, individual companies even though they want to take a stance, they can't act. We want legislation, a bill to enforce that effort, to become the voice and become the governing body for the people in China who cannot speak right now.

Mr. SMITH. Ms. Chai, I will commit to you that we will draft a code of conduct bill and move it forward—hopefully it can be enacted—that hopefully will be a backdrop, like the—I mentioned the Sullivan Principles which were transformational in South Africa as to how U.S. corporations that did business in that apartheid land could only do it if they were completely separated from that egregious policy of racism.

Ms. CHAI. If that bill can be drafted sooner, next week. I am coming back for a CEO Forum and they will be very interested to hear that.

Mr. SMITH. Lamar Smith, the distinguished chairman of the Judiciary Committee, was here before and has joined on as a cosponsor of H.R. 2121 which would deny visas to those individuals who are complicit in these violations of human rights, including forced abortion and involuntary sterilization. I know that you met with him, and you persuaded him—he is a very, very fine chairman—to become a cosponsor, and the bill was referred to his committee. So I am very grateful for that, on your behalf. Ms. Buerkle.

Ms. BUERKLE. Thank you, Mr. Chairman, and thank you to our witnesses today. I apologize for being late. I am a nurse and I am an attorney, but I am also the mother of six children and four of them are daughters. You just get a knot in the pit of your stomach as you listen to this.

I recently was honored with the designation of being the Congressional Delegate to the U.N. So I would like to see how we could—not just today but ongoing—take your information and be able to work with it through the U.N. Recently, a couple of weeks ago, our chairwoman, Ileana Ros-Lehtinen, introduced legislation that would reform the U.N., which would look at how we spend American taxpayers' dollars, and we don't want to spend that money if it goes against the principles of the United States of America.

And this flies in the face of the principles of the United States of America. So I would like to take that role, along with this legislation that we introduced a couple of weeks ago, and push this further to see what we can accomplish that way, especially getting more information, holding China accountable through the U.N. and certainly with this piece of legislation. So I would like to talk further. We will get your information so we can do that.

I guess my first question is, where are the feminists? Where are the feminists who are so concerned about women's rights?

Ms. CHAI. We don't know. But they still have a chance to do something. And I do have a suggestion, Congresswoman Buerkle, regarding the UNFPA funding. I see the two sides cannot reach agreement right now. Chairman Smith is leading the effort to defund the UNFPA and President Obama's side is going to be potentially vetoing the funding. So we would like to propose a third option. I think that might be a great chance of hope to end gendercide, particularly in China, is to modify the UNFPA funding into funding that would end gendercide. We—at All Girls Allowed—have started a 1-year pilot program. Basically we give women who give birth to girls $240 a year, $20 per month for a year. To give her dignity, give her respect, let her know how to cherish the baby girl she is holding in her arms so she doesn't have to, you know, abandon the baby girl or be forced to give up the baby girl.

We have seen a remarkable response. And the mothers would give us letters and feedback saying, it was through this program that their heads were lifted up, and they took pride in their baby girls in their arms and their husbands started showing respect for them, their in-laws started showing respect to them and the entire community started taking a different look at women who gave birth to girls. Just $20 a month, for those families who earn under $2 a day, which is 468 million Chinese people living today in massive level of poverty, that is a significant amount of resource. So if that $50 million can be sent to China or India—you know, divide it in whatever way they want, and encourage the Chinese Government, we would have so much money to match 10 to 1. Then we are talking about $550 million.

We recently spoke to a diplomat from Japan. They are very sensitive to the rising military expansion of China by the single branches, and also the hostility and nationalism toward Japan and neighboring countries. So they are interested in joining the U.S. effort, if that three-way can be done. Basically the U.S. would reform the UNFPA to stop using that funding to support forced abortions, but use that money to give and receive a baby girl's right to life. And you know to have the Chinese Government to join the programs and to give them the chance to do something good. And to have the Japanese Government participate in this community and effort.

And if that kind of money can be given to 2–3 million families who are going to give birth to baby girls, I believe in 1 year China's gendercide can be ended. Then we would come back and say, what can we do with the 37 million single men? I believe something can be done. I would appreciate your feedback and your efforts.

Ms. BUERKLE. Thank you. We would be very interested, yes, in talking about the program and looking to see what we can do to help.

Ms. CHAI. Yes. I spoke to Speaker Boehner's policy adviser, Katherine Haley this morning, and she encouraged us. She said, you know, suggest that in the hearing and see whether we can have a breakthrough, a creative way to make good happen. So I thank you for your time.

Ms. BUERKLE. Thank you.

Ms. LITTLEJOHN. Representative Buerkle, I wanted to respond to your question about the U.N. Two things: Number one, Women's Rights Without Frontiers has submitted an extensive complaint to the U.N. several months ago about forced abortion in China. And I just got an e-mail from them about a week ago saying that they are forwarding it to the nation of China. So we will see what happens with that. Number two, I participated in the U.N. CSW week of—the conference that they give every year. But the issue of forced abortion in China was nowhere on the agenda, and my presentation was not even a side event. It was like a side-side event. And yet it is something that affects one out of every five women in the world, and it is the biggest just numerically perpetrator of violence against women in the world is this one thing.

So if there is anything that you could do to raise the visibility of the issue so that we could discuss the one-child policy, maybe even at a side event or maybe even in the plenary session of the U.N. CSW conference, that would just be great.

Ms. BUERKLE. Very good. We can talk about that and we will strategize a little more and we will get your cards and your contact information.

Oftentimes you hear the apologists saying that the vast majority of the Chinese agree with this policy. Can you just comment on that. And then I don't want to hold up the chairman, but I will yield back.

Ms. CHAI. During the 1989 movement, right before that, we were told, the majority of Chinese people don't care about politics, don't want freedom, don't want democracy. And we know what happened. They were willing to give their lives for that freedom. And I believe the majority of Chinese are willing to give their lives to have the freedom of their body, of their marriage, and of their peace back, if they are allowed to. If they are being given the chance, they are not fighting alone. And I believe that day will come.

Ms. BUERKLE. Thank you.

Ms. LITTLEJOHN. I was interviewed this morning on Voice of America which was broadcast into China, Taiwan, and Hong Kong. And I spoke about the one-child policy. This is the fourth or the fifth time that I have spoken on Voice of America directly into the nation of China about the one-child policy. And the comments that I get back—because people can call in with comments and questions. I would say the vast majority of them are highly critical of the policy. I think that it is hard to gauge what the majority believe in China because they are not free to speak. You go over to China and as a tourist and say, Well, what do you think about the one-child policy? Do you expect that person to actually take the risk of getting detained for revealing State secrets by saying, you know what I have been a victim of forced abortions three times and I think it is the most appalling thing in the world? They can't talk about it. They are not free to voice their dissent.

Ms. BUERKLE. Thank you very much. I will look forward to our conversation following the hearing. I yield back.

Mr. SMITH. Thank you very much, Ms. Buerkle. Let me just conclude with a few final questions. First to Ms. Ji and Ms. Liu and

Chai Ling as well because we have three people on this panel who have suffered forced abortions. If you could just briefly speak—we know about the 500 women per day who commit suicide in China. Ms. Liu mentioned earlier that she almost committed suicide. And I am wondering, the mental health, the emotional downside to—or the consequences of this horrific policy, how do the women endure this? I mean broken marriages, the chemical dependencies of various kinds or just—how do the women endure this? Do they go numb?

Ms. LIU I became very depressed. I just wanted to close up inside the home. I didn't want to go out.

As a mother, when I became pregnant, I had this motherly instinct to protect and save my children. My baby literally had to be yanked out of my body. In addition to the physical pain, I experienced this terrible sense of guilt and shame that I somehow failed my child and was not able to protect my child and was not able to, you know, give life. I failed at being a mother. I felt so deeply guilty, as if I had killed my own children with my own hands.

Mr. SMITH. Is it commonplace for the women, even though they have been coerced into the abortion, to take the guilt onto themselves?

Ms. LIU Even though I mentally knew in my mind that I was forced, somehow I still internalized that guilt and that probably explains why I direct anger and resentment toward my husband.

In China, for the people who have wealth, have money, have connections to power, they can have a second child and they can have more if they want or choose to.

Mr. SMITH. By paying a bribe?

Ms. CHAI. They can pay fines, they can pay bribes, and they could find ways to have their babies in America. She felt as a worker, a normal average worker, she had no way to protect her own children and that further gave her that sense of helplessness in that kind of society.

I felt so deeply shamed, as if I—you know, in my culture, I felt like I had failed my father, I had failed my family. And I felt that I would become a woman to be pointed at on the street, in a public corner or square, to be shamed, to display my guilt, whatever things I have done that led to the pregnancy. In my book, I write about my growing up and how, when I was a young child in grade school, I was goofing around with a classmate when we were supposed to study. And the teacher came in, dragged a poor boy to the front of the classroom and just beat the heck out of the poor boy.

I was terrified. I thought, well, next he is going to go after me. Then when he stopped, he looked at me and he said, we have three classes of people. The first class we teach with eyes. The second class people we teach with words. And the third class of people we teach with our fist. And it was internalizing that—it was because of that experience I promised myself—I prayed to God, even though I didn't know God at that time, I wanted to be an outstanding kid. I would never want to be the third class of people that would be taught with fists. So when I got pregnant and when I realized I had really failed my family, that I was going to bring disgrace to my family, it was a fear of being exposed that rushed all of that to the forced abortion clinics. Even though I came to a free country, when I met Reggie—again, as I said in the book.

Ms. LITTLEJOHN. You can talk about it.

Ms. CHAI. Thank you for the permission. I started realizing, oh, my gosh, this could be four lives. And I could have four babies. I sat down with my American husband and I felt like I had to confess to him. And at that moment, I just felt such a deep sense of pain and it was so deep I just couldn't stop crying. Of course, he got up from where I was and went to finish his e-mail. And as I was writing, finishing the book—and I still felt so afraid to share my own experience—I prayed and it was just miraculous. A sister called Wan did not know me, yet God made her hear my prayer the next day. She decided to connect with All Girls Allowed and she just started telling me her own abortion experience, very similar. She was in college. A similar situation where the boyfriend's father took her to the abortion. When she started to realize what was going on, she felt so shamed and she was so afraid to tell anybody. For whatever reason, she decided to tell me. I listened to her story. I said thank you very much. And I didn't tell her my story because I was still so under the shame.

So this is the first time you are hearing about it. And I know a few of my friends in the Chinese community read my manuscript and they were shocked. So the culture is being so—I don't want to say brainwashed and also saturated with abortion culture, with a culture that does not know the Creator, nor cherish the creation. It is a culture that values so much the goods and products more than humans. And it continues being made through violence to violence, through war to war.

Mr. SMITH. A culture of death.

Ms. CHAI. Yes.

Mr. SMITH. Let me just ask two final questions and then any final concluding comments you have. Let me just say, it is in China's own self-interest to abandon this abomination called the one-child-per-couple policy and yet many at the U.N., many in the U.S. and now increasingly in Africa we are seeing that there is not only support and enabling of it, but there is an embrace of it that maybe we need it here. I would point out to the committee that you go back to the genesis of child limitation. Margaret Sanger, the founder of Planned Parenthood, actually wrote a book called "Child Limitations" in which she admonishes the world to adopt a very small family.

And she even wrote in one of her books called "The Pivot of Civilization," in chapter five, that it is cruel—she called it the cruelty of charity to help poor, indigent women have babies because then you get more of "them," whatever "them" is, whether it be someone of a certain socioeconomic situation or ethnicity. She didn't like Africans. She didn't like Asians. She didn't like Catholics. She didn't like Italians or Irish. It is all in her books. And we need less of them as a direct result.

That mindset is antithetical to human rights and the respect for human rights is now being adopted and is mainstreamed through the U.N. through the Obama administration—and I say that with enormous sadness because the opportunity to be a beacon of hope for the people of China has not evaporated, but it has alluded this White House.

So it is in China's own interest, and I hope they take seriously the admonitions of their own demographers and certainly what this panel and the work of Dr. Hudson and others have done to bring focus to their impending economic implosion directly attributable to the one-child-per-couple policy. It may take some years but it is going to happen. So I am amazed that as smart as so many people are in that government—because you know, it is not monolithic. There are people who hopefully see it for what it is. It is not only cruel to women and children and to men, but it is also sewing the seeds of their own demise economically.

But let me just ask about sex trafficking. I was chagrinned that the administration did not include China as a Tier III, egregious violator of sex trafficking. I wrote that law. If ever there was a country that ought to be on Tier III and, therefore, subject to sanctions, it is the People's Republic of China, not only for what they do in North Korea where North Korean women are sold into slavery, those lucky ones that make it across the border. But there has been an exponential rise of trafficking in China itself because of the missing girls.

It is inevitable, given the fact that this policy has that kind of consequence. Your thoughts? Perhaps Reggie, you want to speak to it. But China is becoming the biggest magnet for sex traffickers in the world today, and it will only get worse. Today Dr. Hudson amended our understanding. You know 40 million men won't be able to find wives by 2020 because they have been exterminated. She said that the number is now 40 to 50 million men who will not be able to find wives. And she made a very good point I think about how, you know, the poor, the unskilled, the illiterate, those who may not be as attractive as somebody else are the ones likely to fall by the wayside and live a life as a "bare branch." On trafficking, if any of you would like to speak on that.

Ms. LITTLEJOHN. I am glad you brought up the issue of the North Korean refugees. They are some of the saddest people in the world. You have these girls who risk their lives coming across the border, thinking they are coming into some kind of freedom. If human rights were worse anywhere in the world, it is North Korea. And then they get snapped up into this sex trafficking trade and they can be raped, they can be beaten. They can be tortured. They can't say anything about it because as soon as they try to appeal to the authorities, the authorities will simply say, oh, you are from North Korea. You are an economic migrant. We are repatriating you. And then to escape North Korea is considered treason, and they can end up in one of the North Korean death camps. So these are some of the most helpless people in the world. Now in terms of why China is a tier-two as opposed to a Tier III, I can't help wondering whether it has something to do with our debt situation. You know?

Mr. SMITH. I would hope that the administration would be sophisticated enough to know that a country that exports products to the tune of over $250 billion in terms of the balance of trade, is as reliant on the United States to send those products as we are for the trade. And it is $1 trillion out of a 14-point what, three or four publicly owned debt. It is a fraction—a significant one—but it is a percentage of all of our debt. And so my thought is, on the economic issue, we give too much credence to the idea that they might stop buying treasury bills and, frankly, it is all the more reason why we should have linked human rights of every stripe, including respect for women who are subjected to forced abortion and children as part of our trade policy. Unfortunately, Bill Clinton delinked it in 1994. But thank you for those comments. Ms. Chai.

Ms. CHAI. Last time we were here on June 13, we went with you to testify against child trafficking in China. It is such a massive problem taking place every day. One parent showed a victim who went to pick up his own daughter at the school and was 15 minutes late and his daughter was trafficked. And then the same day, I got a $50 bill for being late 15 minutes at my kids' school, and I was so grateful. This man's whole life changed, lost his job, had to sell his house and property to find funding to go on this nationwide campaign to find his daughter. And this kind of action took place every day. And it is being reported that up to 200,000 children and girls are being trafficked every year. And through our report in one of the cities inside China in Fujian where they have 3 million residents, 100,000 to up to 600,000 may be victims of child trafficking.

It is child trafficking, as young girls are trafficked at a young age, as young as even 3 years old to be sold into a family that would raise this girl up to marry their own son because they don't want their son to become one of the 37 million single branches. And that is how these families are taking matters into their own hands. So yes, we would love to have the U.S. leaders' attention and laws to help mediate those situations.

Mr. SMITH. Thank you. Is there anything else that any of our distinguished witnesses would like to add? I would just like to add one other thing maybe as a question or you might want to comment on.

Ms. Liu, you mentioned how your husband was incarcerated. In the 1990s, I chaired a hearing that Harry Wu helped facilitate where we heard from a woman from Fujian province who actually ran one of the family planning centers. She was given a pseudonym, Mrs. Gao, because she was fearful of retaliation against her family and extended family still in China. And she said, by night, she was a wife and mother, and during the day, she was a monster. She self-described as a monster. And she told us that the family planning cadres and the police in their employ had more power to coerce, to arrest, to incarcerate, to beat. And I am wondering, you know, one of the other untold stories is the fact that the jails of China, and especially the detention centers, are failed with men and women, fathers, mothers, when a woman does resist, who are trying to get that woman to go into the abortion mill for a "voluntary abortion." Coercion of every stripe and layer being imposed upon her. She told stories that as late as 9 months gestation, babies, very, very late, just about to be born, children, that women would be pleading with her, Please let me have my baby. And to no avail. And they would hold husbands, fathers until she voluntarily submitted to the abortion. Is that commonplace when a woman resists?

Ms. CHAI. Ms. Liu said, this kind of punishment is very common. In the city, mostly its the family members of these kinds of parents who refuse to give into the forced abortion. They are defiant, trying to keep their babies; then these family members end up being incarcerated into a study class where they are not allowed to go home. And then they will be detained and tormented and continue to go through these kinds of "studies" until they are in compliance with government procedures. In the countryside, it is most common that they just use a tractor to demolish people's houses.

Ms. LITTLEJOHN. By the way, that is all in my report. I have got documentation and photographs of exactly these things. The demolition of houses and the people in the jail cells, the parents and all that in the jail cells. It is all documented and I think it is all current.

Mr. SMITH. Ms. Littlejohn, thank you for documenting that. I look forward to reading your report. Like I said, it will be made a part of the record. Anything else anyone would like to add? Let me again conclude by asking the administration, the Obama administration to finally cease its silence—and that is at best—and its enabling of this great crime against women and children. The Kemp-Kasten language is still the law of the land, that any organization that supports or co-manages a coercive population control program is denied funding. This administration has misapplied that clear nonambiguous law and has provided $50 million a year to the UNFPA, the U.N. population fund. And the situation on the fund vis-à-vis UNFPA and its complete following of Chinese law and regulation has not changed one bit.

And I would read very briefly one paragraph from John Negroponte's findings which he did on behalf of the Bush administration previously and that is that China's birth limitation program relies on harshly coercive measures. He points out that there is a so-called social maintenance fee or social compensation. There are several rewards for couples who adhere to the birth limitation laws, including monthly stipends. So they get preferential treatment if they adhere to it. But he also says that couples who do not comply are penalized by denial of these benefits. According to provincial regulations, social maintenance fees—in other words, you get penalized if you have a child out of the birth allowed regime—are fined from one-half to 10 times the average worker's annual disposable income.

Those who violate the child limit policy by having an unapproved child or helping another to do so may also face disciplinary measures such as job loss or demotion loss of promotion opportunity and other administrative punishments, including as you just said, Ms. Littlejohn, the destruction of property, the bulldozing of homes. We call on the administration, the State Department to have at least some semblance of the human rights policy and stop giving money to those groups that have a hand-in-glove relationship with the Chinese dictatorship.

I thank you for bearing witness to the truth. Your testimony has been very powerful. Yes?

Ms. CHAI. I do want to end this session with hope. I want you all to look at that woman who is there. Her name is Nie Lina. And this past May 2010, we got this call from China that this woman was detained and was scheduled to go for a forced abortion. And people would ask, if President Obama does not do anything, if the U.S. leaders do not do anything, what can we do? And I happened to—it was at 5:00, 5:30, I was watching my daughter's soccer practice. I said you know what, we can do something. We can pray. So we sent an urgent prayer letter to all our prayer warriors. And we prayed. We prayed for God to put his power into these officials' hearts to stop this crime. Forty-eight hours later, that woman was released. So I just want to end this by saying that hope and rescue are on their way. And with time, women will be set free. Thank you.

Mr. SMITH. The hearing is adjourned. Thank you.

[Whereupon, at 4:46 p.m., the subcommittee was adjourned.]

APPENDIX

SUBCOMMITTEE HEARING NOTICE
COMMITTEE ON FOREIGN AFFAIRS
U.S. HOUSE OF REPRESENTATIVES
WASHINGTON, D.C. 20515-0128

SUBCOMMITTEE ON AFRICA, GLOBAL HEALTH, AND HUMAN RIGHTS
Christopher H. Smith (R-NJ), Chairman

September 21, 2011

You are respectfully requested to attend an OPEN hearing of the Subcommittee on Africa, Global Health, and Human Rights, to be held in **Room 2200 of the Rayburn House Office Building (and available live, via the WEBCAST link on the Committee website at http://www.hcfa.house.gov):**

DATE: Thursday, September 22, 2011

TIME: 2:00 p.m.

SUBJECT: China's One-Child Policy: The Government's Massive Crime Against
                   Women and Unborn Babies

WITNESSES: Ms. Chai Ling
                   Founder
                   All Girls Allowed

                   Ms. Reggie Littlejohn
                   Founder and President
                   Women's Rights Without Frontiers

                   Valerie Hudson, Ph.D
                   Professor
                   Department of Political Science
                   Brigham Young University

                   Ms. Ji Yequig
                   Victim of forced abortion

                   Ms. Liu Ping
                   Victim of forced abortion

By Direction of the Chairman

The Committee on Foreign Affairs seeks to make its facilities accessible to persons with disabilities. If you are in need of special accommodations, please call 202/225-5021 at least four business days in advance of the event, whenever practicable. Questions with regard to special accommodations in general (including availability of Committee materials in alternative formats and assistive listening devices) may be directed to the Committee

COMMITTEE ON FOREIGN AFFAIRS

MINUTES OF SUBCOMMITTEE ON _____*Africa, Global Health, and, Human Rights*_____ HEARING

Day____*Thursday*____Date__*Septemeber 22, 2011*__Room___*2200 Rayburn*___

Starting Time ____*2:00 p.m.*____ Ending Time ___*4:46 p.m.*___

Recesses __*0*__ (____to ____) (____to ____) (____to ____) (____to ____) (____to ____) (____to ____)

Presiding Member(s)

Rep. Chris Smith

Check all of the following that apply:

Open Session ☑   Electronically Recorded (taped) ☑
Executive (closed) Session ☐   Stenographic Record ☑
Televised ☑

TITLE OF HEARING:

China's One-Child Policy: The Government's Massive Crime Against Women and Unborn Babies

---

SUBCOMMITTEE MEMBERS PRESENT:

Rep. Chris Smith, Rep. Jeff Fortenberry, Rep. Ann Marie Buerkle

---

NON-SUBCOMMITTEE MEMBERS PRESENT: *(Mark with an * if they are not members of full committee.)*

Rep. Lamar Smith*

HEARING WITNESSES: Same as meeting notice attached? Yes ☑ No ☐
(If "no", please list below and include title, agency, department, or organization.)

STATEMENTS FOR THE RECORD: *(List any statements submitted for the record.)*

Prepared statement from Ms. Chai Ling
Prepared statement from Ms. Reggie Littlejohn
Prepared statement from Dr. Valerie Hudson
Prepared statement from Ms. Ji Yequig
Prepared statement from Ms. Liu Ping
Women's Rights Without Fronteiers report

TIME SCHEDULED TO RECONVENE _____
or
TIME ADJOURNED ____*4:46 p.m.*____

Subcommittee Staff Director

Post Office Box 54401, San Jose, CA 95154, 310.592.5722
www.womensrightswithoutfrontiers.org

China's One Child Policy: New Evidence of Coercion
Forced Abortion, Sterilization, Contraception
And the Practice of "Implication"

Reggie Littlejohn, President
Women's Rights Without Frontiers
September 22, 2011
House Committee on Foreign Affairs,
Subcommittee on Africa, Global Health, and Human Rights

EXCERPTS – To read the entire report, please visit
www.womensrightswithoutfrontiers.org

**Case Two: Family Planning Officials of Nanzhan Town, Wenshang County,
Shandong Province detain and torture a couple for reporting for a pregnancy
check-up one day late.**

When: August 20, 2009. 11:30AM
Where: Nanzhan Town, Wenshang County, Shangdong Province
Source: club.china.com

Here is the account in the words of the victim:

My name is Xiangan Zhao. My wife is Xiaoyan Li. We both come from Caoliu Village,
Nanzhan Town, Wenshang County, Shandong Province. Both of us were working in
Yantai City to make a living. We were beaten and illegally detained by the Family
Planning Officials of Nanzhan Town Family Planning Office simply because we were
one day late to report for a pregnancy check-up. [Every married woman who doesn't stay
in her hometown, like this victim who works at another city, has to come back to her
hometown regularly for a pregnancy check-up—required periodically to determine
whether a woman is illegally pregnant].   I phoned the police for help several times. Not

only did the police refuse to help, but they told us: "It is legal for the Family Planning Officials to do that. It's not our responsibility to deal with that!"

Shengbo Zhou (Vice Town Head), Zhihong Hu (head of the Family Planning Office), Changrui Yin (middle-level leader) and other leaders were all involved in beating us. All the Family Planning Officials were present as well.

Shandong is notorious for violent family planning. Nevertheless, suffering so much simply because of reporting for a pregnancy check-up one day late is beyond my imagination.

My wife, Xiaoyan Li, and I were living in Gongjiadao Residents' Committee, Zhichu street, Zhifu District, Yantai City, Shandong Province. We had all the legal certificates required by the "Regulations of Family Planning for Floating Population." At noon of August 6, 2009, we received a phone call from Airong Liu (head of the women's federation of Caoliu Village, Nanzhan Town, Wenshang County, Shandong Province, which is the location of our registered residence). She informed us that we needed to report for a pregnancy check-up. My wife went to the designated hospital of Zhifu District, Yantai City to check and obtained the certificate issued by the hospital to the local Family Planning Department. My wife requested to send the certificate report to the Family Planning Department of Nanzhan Town, Wenshang County through their network (the specialized official network of Family Planning Departments). The report, however, could not be sent due to network issues. So the Family Planning Official phoned Zhihong Hu (the head of Nanzhan Town Family Planning Office). He approved my wife's request to send the report after the network issues were resolved. He also confirmed that there was no need for my wife to go back to our hometown for another pregnancy check-up. The local Family Planning Office sent the report at noon on August 12, 2009, after the network had returned to normal. However, Airong Liu phoned us at noon on August 18, 2009. She told us that the report sent through network was invalid and asked us to return for another pregnancy check-up immediately. Shengbo Zhou (the Town officer in charge of family planning) agreed. But we were delayed by something urgent for one day. We took the train back on the evening of August 19 and arrived at 10:30 in the morning of August 20. We rested at home for one hour and phoned Airong Liu. She said, "Everyone is waiting for you. We'll pull down your house if you don't come." Because we were late for one day and were not clear about what she meant, we hurried to the Family Planning Office to report for the check-up. While my wife was receiving the check-up, I explained the reason for being late to Airong Liu politely. But she shouted at me: "What? Are you hoping that I will pay your travel expenses as well?"

At that time, an official with long hair and long face (his name is Changrui Yin) came downstairs from the second floor and said, "Beat him. He has so many excuses for being late." Then he took the lead in beating me. Many people followed him and struck me down. They beat and kicked like storms. When I tried to stand up and run away by instinct, he commanded again, "Beat him with rubber sticks." I was stricken down again and could not move this time. They dragged my arms and threw me in a dark room (the second room on the east side of the door of the Family Planning Office).

Then he gave another command: "Go and beat his wife." My wife had just finished the check-up at that time . He dragged her off the bed to hit her. He said, "This is for your coming late!" My wife said, "Director Hu told me there was no need to come back for another check-up." We never thought this statement would irritate him. He shouted: "You have a good reason for being late, don't you? Take her in the room!" So the Family Planning Official dragged my wife into a dark room and beat her brutally. She gripped their legs and knelt down to beg, "I know I'm wrong. Please forgive me. Please forgive me......" They finally stopped hitting after she begged for a while. Her whole body was already covered with wounds then.

They checked the items we carried (they worried that we were taking cameras or other devices to record their brutal behavior) and detained us in the same room. They sealed the door and the window closely. One person guarded outside the door. Then I found there were already eight or nine people in the room. I felt sharp pain throughout my whole body. My wounds got more serious at about two o' clock in the afternoon and I had difficulty breathing, so my wife begged the guard to allow me out for treatment. He reported to his superior and in the end they approved. They gave my cell phone back to me (it fell out of my pocket when I was beaten). I couldn't walk and my wife was unable to bear me on her back, so she requested the Family Planning Office to drive me to the hospital, but they did not respond. My wife had to phone the police for help. She described our situation and location, but something surprising happened......After the Family Planning Officials knew that we phoned the police, they grabbed my cell phone and detained us again. The Police Station was only about 100 meters from the Family Planning Office, but the policemen never came to help us.

Our family came to the Family Planning Office six hours after we left home. They reported to the police again at the sight of our wounds. This time two policemen (they did not wear the police uniform) came and said: "It's legal for the Family Planning Officials to do this. It's not our responsibility to deal with it!" Then the two policemen mediated with the Family Planning Officials. In the end, the Family Planning Officials sent us to the town People's Hospital but left without paying a single cent of the medical fee.

Later the Nanzhan Town police station refused to provide us with a Judicial Expertise Certificate. [Note: this Certificate is from a medical expert, who will determine the extent of the victim's injuries, to be considered by a judge in rendering a verdict.] So my relatives sent an informants' letter to the head of the Province through email. The relatives sent a document to Nanzhan Family Planning Office after they knew our experiences. Our problem, however, was never resolved. Without any legal assistance, we had to go to the Nanzhan Family Planning Office at noon of the 23rd to negotiate a settlement. Shengbo Zhou (Vice head of the Town) and Zhihong Hu (Director of Nanzhan Family Planning Office) said, "There is no need to sue us because no one will care about your case. The Head of the Province will never send anyone to deal with it, nor will he deal with it on his own. All the documents are left here for us to handle. Have a look if you don't believe my words. Documents from the Provincial Government are all here. On the other hand, even if you win the lawsuit, we will take revenge on your relatives. We agree to cover seventy percent of the medical fee and that's it."

. . . .

I was afraid they may continue to beat me in the hospital, so I left the hospital and went back to Yantai secretly. But since that time I have been left with sequelae [pathology resulting from trauma]. I have a partial loss of work ability and I cannot do heavy labor to this day.

I'd like to ask: where is the justice? Where is the law? Where is the Party discipline? We want justice for the unreasonable beating and illegal detention. They must pay for the medical fee, nursing fee, travelling expenses and compensate for loss of working time, emotional damages and so on.

I have a sound recording of Zhihong Hu (Director of the Family Planning Office) as evidence. I also have photos of our wounds and the certificate of the pregnancy check-up.
When: August 20, 2009.
Where: Nanzhan Town Wenshang County Shandong Province
Source: club.china.com

Case Seven: The Family Planning Office of Zaoshi Sub-District Office, Leiyang City, Hunan Province struck a man in the head, permanently disabling him.

When: March 7, 2008
Where: Zaoshi Sub-District Office, Leiyang City, Hunan Province
Source: Interview by the Chinese Author, posted on
http://www.tianya.cn/publicforum/content/news/1/93996.shtml

Xin Liu (male, 32 years old, Level Seven Permanently Disabled) [Note: in China there are different degrees of disability. Level Seven is very high.] comes from the "eighth group" of Douling village, Daheyu Township, Leiyang city, Hunan Province. He lives in Liujia alley, Zaoshi village committee, Zaoshi Sub-District Office, Leiyang city. His wife Binglan Yang gave birth to a second child at the end of 2007.

At about eight o' clock in the evening of March 7, 2008, Changzheng Luo (Vice Secretary of Zaoshi Sub-District Office) headed about thirty [Family Planning] Officials (most of them were local rogues) to Xin Liu's home and urged him to open the door. Xiandong Luo, Xin's elder sister's husband who lived next door heard the sound and hurried out. When asked what they were coming for, the Officials answered: "We are here to collect the Social Compensation Fee for your extra child. Open the door, or else we will break in!"

On hearing that, Xing Liu (Xin's younger brother) also got up from bed. He walked up to the door and asked them for their identification. They refused to reveal their identities and just kept threatening. Later Xing recognized that one tall man was from Zaoshi Sub-

District Office, and asked: "Are you working in Zaoshi Sub-District Office?" He answered, "Yes." So Xing opened the door.

Changzheng Luo rushed in with those Officials. He dragged Xin's wife, Binglan Yang, and asked her to pay the fine for her extra child. Xin asked them to show their credentials and enforce the law in a civilized manner, but he was immediately met with a brutal mass brawl. At this sight, Xiandong Luo said, "No hitting!" but he was beaten as well. His face was smashed and broken by their weapon. Blood streamed down his face.

Afterwards, the man beating Xiandong Luo turned round and hit Xin's temple with a glass bottle. Xin was stunned immediately and fell down on the ground. Blood streamed across his body. Xin's mother (over seventy years old) laid down and held him with her arms, but they kicked her abdomen. Xin's younger brother's wife locked the door and intended to report to the police.

They asked her to open the door and let them leave. She refused and was slapped. Then they forced her to hand over the key.

At this sight, Xing ran out of the house and called the police. After a while six policemen from Leiyang bureau of public security arrived. Seeing that Xin was laying on the ground and bleeding, the policemen suggested rescuing him. However, Changzheng Luo commanded the policemen not to.

Then Xin's elder brother arrived. He knelt down in front of Changzheng Luo together with his old mother, begging him to rescue Xin. Wangai Xu who was looking on in the beginning called the SOS. [This is the Chinese equivalent of 911.] Xin was carried into the ambulance by his brothers while Changzheng Luo stalked off with all the rogues.

Xin Liu and Xiandong Luo are both in hospital for treatment now. They had to pay all their own medical fees. [Since this report was written, they were released from the hospital, but Xin Liu suffers from permanent disability.]

Case Eight: Family Planning Officials of Wutong Town, Yongtai County, Fuzhou City, Fujian Province forcibly abort eight and a half month twins.

When: December 13, 2007
Where: Wutong Town, Yongtai County, Fuzhou City, Fujian Province
Source: http://bbs.fzbm.com/simple/?t601651.html This author is a journalist who interviewed the victims.

On December 13, 2007, Mrs. Dong (34 years old) from Wutong Town, Yongtai County, Fuzhou City was pregnant with unplanned twin babies for almost nine months. She was working in Ganzhe Town, Minhou County, Fuzhou Province together with her husband. Unfortunately, her pregnancy was discovered by the local Family Planning Office. At about two o' clock in the afternoon she was taken to the local health center forcibly.

Without the agreement or signature of Mrs. Dong or her family, she was held by more than ten people and injected Ethacridine Lactate at about five o' clock. The Family Planning Officials declared that they would be responsible for any death. The twin babies struggled for a long time in their mother's uterus and died in the end. Until half past nine in the evening of December 14, she was still waiting to induce the dead babies. The local government blocked the event tightly and forbade anyone from interviewing the victim. Until now her health condition is still unknown . . .

Case Nine: Jining Family Planning Department pulled down a mother's house and forced a pregnant woman to abort during the eighth month of pregnancy.

When: Winter, 2007
Where: Jining City, Rencheng County, Shangdong Province
Source: bbs.sina.com.cn

In [winter, 2007] the Family Planning Office of Ershilipu town, Rencheng County, Jining city launched a Family Planning law enforcement inspection campaign. The Family Planning Office pulled down houses and caught women with illegal pregnancies. Moreover, a woman was compelled to abort her eight-month pregnancy. Before the operation, the doctor touched the baby in her abdomen and sighed: "The bone is already hard, already a human." . . . There was no opportunity to take photos of the forced abortion because of the Officials' violent interference.

Case Twelve: Family Planning Officials beat fifty-year-old father in Pizhou city.

When: October 11, 2006
Where: Beixi Village, Gangshang Town, Pizhou Xuzhou City
Source: http://www.pzzc.net/simple/?t159438.html

October 11, 2006 was the day of crushing despair for Shenyue Zhang's family. Because it was on this day that Shenyue Zhang was beaten to death by the Family Planning Officials.

Shenyue Zhang (fifty years old) lived in Beixi village, Gangshang town, Pizhou city, Jiangsu province. He was an honest farmer with strong body and loud voice. He was good at farm work. He had two sons. His older son got married and had a lovely son. The couple worked in another city all through the year, so all the burdens of the farming work fell on Zhang's shoulders. He was satisfied with his life, although it was bitter sometimes. However, at about ten o' clock in the morning of October 10, 2009, Family Planning Officials of Gangshang Town came to his family. They said his family was in violation of the Family Planning Policy because his son was suspected of having an extra child. They took him to the town Family Planning Office forcibly and detained him in a small room. His family members went there to send him food several times but couldn't get in. His fourth younger brother Shenhai Zhang said: "His son and daughter-in-law work in another city all the year round and they have no plan for another child. But according to the regulation of the town government, women of childbearing age must submit to a pregnancy exam every two months. His daughter-in-law planned to submit to the exam on October 5th, but was delayed because of her job. That's one reason why they seized him. But the more important reason is that they wanted to get some money on this trumped-up charge." However, this time what he lost was not money.

Shenyue Zhang was seized at about ten o' clock in the morning of October 10. At about three o' clock in the afternoon of the next day, Shenchang Zhang (head of village public security) and Shenyou Zhang (one of the village group leaders) came to his family and told his fourth younger brother Shenhai Zhang: "He was injured in the Family Planning Office. (Actually, he had died.) Secretary Zhang and Secretary Kong of the Gangshang Town Party Committee invite you there for a conversation."

Shenhai went to the town government with them and knew that his brother had died at midnight. Secretary Zhang said: "The dead can't revive. Your brother's body has been sent to Pizhou city. Go back home and talk with your family. The government will take your needs into consideration." Shenhai and his family went to the town government several times, asking to have a look at his brother's body, but were all stopped outside. Until now he still doesn't know where his brother's body is.

The whole family hated what the Family Planning Office had done. The government put off their solicitations again and again. Shenhai felt that the government seemed to be intentionally hiding and postponing. So his family sat quietly in front of the government office building to protest and ask them to deal with his brother's death promptly. But the government stopped using the office building and kept the door locked. The government officials were nowhere to be found. There was nobody in the Family Planning Office.

Shenhai Zhang was heart-broken about his brother's death. He said, "According to the local custom, I will hold a memorial ceremony for my brother who was persecuted to death. I have no choice but to set up the mourning hall in front of the government and burn joss sticks as well as paper money to comfort my brother. I don't need any compensation. I will do whatever I can to punish the murderer, even if I have to report to Beijing!" Tears ran out of his eyes as he spoke, because in his heart his elder brother is as respectable as his father.

According to Wei, Town Party Committee Commissary in charge of publicity, Shenyue Zhang was taken to the Family Planning Office to clarify himself. He was put up for the night because there were too many things to ask him. But he hanged himself at mid-night.

The case has been escalated to the City People's Procuratorate for further investigation. The result will be published soon. In a statement, Shenyue Zhang's fourth younger brother said: "Is there any exception that the town Family Planning Office didn't seize people forcibly at all? You beat people for no reason every time. Two years ago one villager was beaten to death by you, isn't that true? You didn't bear any legal liability, but only paid 7,000 [Yuan, or approximately $1097] for his death and that's it. This time, why didn't you preserve the crime scene? Instead, you destroyed the evidence. Why didn't you allow us to have a look at my brother's body?" Immediately he [the Family Planning Officer] was struck dumb.

Shenhai Zhang asked three times: "Was my elder brother in violation of the Family Planning policy?" But he [the Family Planning Officer, Wei] kept silent. He could not give an answer. The two sides all stuck to their own positions. At this moment, it was no longer a government that helped the people deal with actual problems. The two sides were just like two groups of different interests. Who knows, while they were fighting, the dead was laying in the deep freezer of the funeral home, unable to be laid to rest!

The power of the Family Planning Office has changed into a money tree.

What's the reason that the town Family Planning officials would rather take the risk of killing and bearing legal liability? Probably Shenhai Zhang's words illuminate us. He said: "Family Planning is a fundamental national policy. But why have many young couples escaped punishment even if they are in violation of the law? The reason is money. No one will care if you pay 4,000 [Yuan, approximately $626 first and another 28,000 [Yuan, approximately $4388] after the childbirth. In the villages the richest people are not the village heads, but the Family Planning Officials."

"If you give birth to an extra child without giving money, the Family Planning Officials will seize, beat and starve your parents and parents-in-law. You will surely try every means to pay to set your family free." On this evidence, not only does the Family Planning work of Gangshang town meet the objectives, but also far exceeds them. They make use of the Family Planning Policy and take illegal measures to make money for themselves and turn the Family Planning Office into a money tree!

Printed in Great Britain
by Amazon.co.uk, Ltd.,
Marston Gate.